Christian Existence

in the

New Testament

Volume I

CHRISTIAN EXISTENCE
IN THE
NEW TESTAMENT

VOLUME I

RUDOLF   SCHNACKENBURG

UNIVERSITY OF NOTRE DAME PRESS

1968

NIHIL OBSTAT: Joseph Hoffman, C.S.C.
Censor Deputatus

IMPRIMATUR: Leo A. Pursley, D.D.
Bishop of Fort Wayne-South Bend
June 12, 1968.

First published as
**CHRISTLICHE EXISTENZ NACH DEM
NEUEN TESTAMENT**
by Kösel-Verlag, Munich

© *1967 by Kösel-Verlag, Munich*

Translated by F. Wieck

Copyright © 1968 by

THE UNIVERSITY OF NOTRE DAME PRESS
Notre Dame, Indiana 46556

Library of Congress Card No. 68-27576

Manufactured in the United States of America

Abbreviations

BZ   *Biblische Zeitschrift*, Neue Folge, Pader-
         born, 1957
LThK   *Lexikon für Theologie und Kirche*, 2nd
         rev. ed., 10 vol., Freiburg i.Br. 1957–1965
RB   *Revue Biblique*, Jerusalem-Paris
ThWNT   *Theologisches Wörterbuch zum Neuen
         Testament*, 8 vols., Stuttgart 1933–1966
         (not yet completed)
ZNW   *Zeitschrift für die neutestamentliche
         Wissenschaft*, Berlin

*Note: The biblical citations are taken from the Revised
Standard Version.*

Contents

I MAN BEFORE GOD—MAN'S IMAGE
   IN THE BIBLE   1

   The Integral View of Man, p. 4; The Bond
   with the Community, p. 12; The Historicity
   of Man, p. 16; Man and His Salvation, p. 23.

II THE PENITENTIAL SERMON IN
   THE NEW TESTAMENT   33

   John the Baptist and His Call for Conversion, p. 37; Christ's Call for Conversion, p.
   43; The Penitential Sermon in the Early
   Church: The Acts of the Apostles, p. 50;
   The Recedence of the Idea of Conversion
   with Paul and John, p. 54; The Final Conversion Sermon in the New Testament; The
   Apocalypse of John, p. 60.

III THE MEANING OF FAITH IN THE BIBLE   67

   The Kinds of Faith in the Bible, p. 70; The
   Life of Faith, p. 83; Unbelief, p. 92.

IV THE IMITATION OF CHRIST   99

   The Original Meaning in Jesus' Own Statements, p. 102; How the Early Church Understood the Imitation of Christ, p. 114; Application to the Christian Situation of Today,
   p. 122.

Contents

V THE SERMON ON THE MOUNT
AND MODERN MAN   128

Inadequate Answers, p. 130; The Sermon on
the Mount in the Framework of Jesus' Message, p. 141; The Sermon on the Mount as a
Guide Today, p. 150.

VI CHRISTIAN PERFECTION ACCORDING
TO MATTHEW   158

The Old Testament Foundation of the Concept of Perfection, p. 162; Perfection According to the Sermon on the Mount, p. 167;
Perfection and the Imitation of Christ: The
Evangelic Counsels, p. 179.

VII THE CONCEPT OF THE WORLD IN
THE NEW TESTAMENT   190

The Historically Decayed and Morally Corrupt World, p. 195; The God-created World
Called to the New Creation, p. 209; The Tension in the Christian's Relation to the
World, p. 221.

Index   229

Man Before God —
Man's Image in the Bible

The problems that arise out of modern man's struggle to maintain his dignity and freedom, his essential selfhood amidst the growing social collectivization of our age, have given a peculiar importance to man's image in the Bible. That image, it is true, stems from a period which is characterized by very different social and economic structures and by much less complex conditions of life; yet it can still reveal to us today, in a valid and convincing manner, the enduring human dimension. The biblical view of man does not disregard man's earthly, historical mode of existence. On the contrary, the Bible regards man, in his creatureliness, as the crown of God's creation in the midst of the created world. He is placed in the current of history and seen as one who must act in history, although history remains subject to God's will. Man's lowliness and greatness, his misery and his glory emerge side by side, and every page in the Bible is concerned with the question of what constitutes man's greatness and how he

1

can find salvation. The answer is plain and simple: by facing God, clinging to God. It may seem paradoxical, but according to the Bible, man understands and achieves his true humanity only when he no longer strives for selfhood but surrenders to another: to the ineffably greater God who is absolutely superior to man. God is the partner of human nature who alone makes man free to achieve his true "humanity." As distinct from other theological approaches, the Bible rests on certain basic assumptions arising from the Semitic turn of mind of its authors—assumptions that come close to modern man's view of himself and his existence; among them in particular the integral concept of man, and the sense of his "historicity."[1] On the

[1] In the history of recent philosophy, the historicity of man has assumed an ever more prominent position, almost as though it were a new discovery. Philosophical discussion shows the extraordinary complexity of the concept and the problems connected with it. For a general orientation see G. Bauer, *Geschichtlichkeit. Wege und Irrwege eines Begriffs* (Berlin, 1963), with an excellent bibliography. On the Biblical concepts of history, see, among others: Karl Löwith, *Weltgeschichte und Heilsgeschehen* (Zurich-Vienna, 1953); J. Daniélou, *The Lord of History* (Chicago, 1958); R. Bultmann, *History and Eschatology* (Edinburgh, 1958); O. Plöger, *Theokratie und Eschatologie* (Neukirchen, 1959); H. W. Wolff, "Das Geschichtsverständnis der alttestamentlichen Prophetie," *Evangelische Theologie* 20 (1960), 218–235; C. A. Simpson, "An Inquiry into the Biblical Theology of History," *Journal of Theological Studies*

other hand, the Bible goes beyond the egocentric and subjective view of existence, by placing man— the whole man, in his historical existence—before the face of God, and giving to his existence a meaning and direction that point beyond himself and his earthly world. These are the decisive viewpoints which will guide the present examination of man's image in the Bible.[2]

12 (1961), 1–13; J. Moltmann, "Exegese und Eschatologie der Geschichte," *Evangelische Theologie* 22 (1962), 31–66; R. A. F. MacKenzie, *Faith and History in the Old Testament* (Minneapolis, 1963); O. Cullman, *Salvation in History* (New York, 1967); A. Darlap, "Die Heilsgeschichte," in *Mysterium Salutis* I, ed. J. Feiner and M. Löhrer (Einsiedeln-Zurich-Cologne, 1965), 3–156 (with references).

[2] From among the rich literature, we may mention: W. G. Kümmel, *Das Bild des Menschen im Neuen Testament* (Zurich, 1948); W. Eichrodt, *Man in the Old Testament* (Chicago, 1951); C. H. Dodd, P. I. Bratsiotis, R. Bultmann, and H. Clavier, *Man in God's Design According to the New Testament* (Newcastle-on-Tyne, 1952); G. Pidoux, L'homme dans l'Ancien Testament (Newchâtel, 1953); J. Schmid, "Anthropologie" in *Lexikon für Theologie und Kirche* I (Freiburg, 1957), 604–615; O. Schilling, *Das biblische Menschenbild* (Cologne, 1961); C. Spicq, *Dieu et l'homme selon le Nouveau Testament* (Paris, 1961); E. Fascher, *Das Menschenbild in biblischer Sicht* (Berlin, 1962); A. Gelin, *L'homme selon la Bible* (Paris, 1962); L. Scheffczyk, *Der Moderne Mensch vor dem biblischen Menschenbild* (Freiburg, 1964).

THE INTEGRAL VIEW OF MAN

In Genesis 2:7 we read, in the pictorial and strongly anthropomorphic language typical of the report of Yahweh's creation of the world and paradise: "Then the Lord God formed man of dust from the ground, and breathed into his nostrils the breath of life; and man became a living being." In this account, man occupies the center of the created world and is closely bound to the earth; the play on the words *adam* ("man"), *adamah* ("earth") is obvious. Man is indeed a being of the earth; "the first man was from the earth, a man of dust" (1 Cor 15:47). But his essential nature, his existence and life, man receives from God who breathes the breath of life into him, and only in this way does man become a "living being." It is true, of course, that a later theology will read from this passage that man is constituted of a body and a soul; but that is not the direction in which the ancient report is tending. Rather, man comes from the hand of God as an integral creature (as "a living being")[3] and the term that is used (*nephesh*—ψυχή) is precisely *not* the word that designates the "soul" as man's "immortal part."[4] Man owes his

[3] This does not mean that man cannot be involved in the evolution of life on earth. Only the step of becoming properly man ("hominization") must be understood, according to revelation, as a creative act of God. Cf. p. Overhage and K. Rahner, *Das Problem der Hominisation* (Freiburg, 1961).

[4] On the concept *nephech*—ψυχή—see L. Köhler, *Theologie des Alten Testaments* (Tübingen, 1956), 129–

4

entire existence to God, who forms him as the most important dweller on the earth which he is to "till and keep." What the ancient report means to stress is this position of man at the center of creation, underlined further by the subsequent story of the garden of Eden—this and man's position in the face of God. Even though man, formed from the earth, is and remains an inhabitant of the earth, he surpasses the rest of creation; God breathes into him his breath of life, and gives him the garden of Eden. Man thus remains under God's care, and subject to God's mandate, command, and call. Man's God-given existence is realized in the face of God.

The same fundamental ideas, although in a different and still more profound and more developed manner, pervade the report of the generation of heaven and earth with which the Bible now opens. Here, in the First Book of Genesis, God creates man as the final and supreme creature and gives him dominion over the earth. But together with man's supreme and dominant position, the Bible stresses that man is referred to God—and more:

132; P. Van Imschoot, *Théologie de l'Ancien Testament* II (Tournai, 1956), 16–26; D. Lys, *Nèphèsch. Histoire de l'âme dans la révélation d'Israël* (Paris, 1959); J. Schmid, "Der Begriff der Seele im Neuen Testament," in *Einsicht und Glaube* (*Festschrift für G. Söhngen*) (Freiburg, 1962), 112–131; G. Dautzenberg, *Sein Leben bewahren.* Ψυχή *in den Herrenworten der Evangelien* (Munich, 1966), with bibliography.

that man is in the likeness and image of God. "So God created man in his own image, in the image of God he created him; male and female he created them" (Gen 1:27). The whole man, including his body, in his corporeal presence, is God's image, although what is meant is hardly his external form, his upright posture, so much as his inner dignity and dominant position. Being the image of God, man is distinguished from the rest of creation, however that may be conceived and interpreted.[5] Once again, the passage can be read to stress the primacy of the spirit over matter; but the report is not intended to underline the dualistic distinction between spirit and matter; its purpose is to give to man, such as he is and in his integral wholeness, first place at the head of all creation, because he is the image of God. The same thought finds poetic expression in the eighth Psalm, and is

[5] Literature: G. Söhngen, "Die biblische Lehre von der Gottebenbildlichkeit des Menschen," in *Die Einheit in der Theologie* (Munich, 1952), 173–211; D. Cairns, *The Image of God in Man* (New York-London, 1953); W. Eltester, *Eikon im Neuen Testament* (Berlin, 1958); J. J. Stamm, *Die Gottebenbildlichkeit des Menschen im Alten Testament* (Zurich, 1959); H. Gross and F. Mussner, "Gottebenbildlichkeit," *LThK* IV, 1087–1090; J. Jervell, *Imago Dei. Gen 1, 26f im Spätjudentum, in der Gnosis und bei Paulus* (Göttingen, 1960); G. C. Berkouwer, *Man, the Image of God* (Grand Rapids, 1962); H. Wildberger, "Das Abbild Gottes, Gen 1, 26–30," *Theologische Zeitschrift* (Basle) 21 (1965), 245–259, 481–501.

echoed and interpreted in Ecclesiasticus 17:1–24.

This integral view of man, who stands before the face of God as man, in all his creatureliness and greatness, is maintained throughout the Bible, including the New Testament.[6] Certain words of Jesus, intended to strengthen his disciples' courage under persecution, are indicative: "Do not fear those who kill the body but cannot kill the soul; rather fear him who can destroy both soul and body in hell" (Mt 10:28). The idea of the "soul" which cannot be killed by the death of the body is strangely transmuted in the sequel, according to which God can destroy the whole man ("soul and body") in hell. "What matters here is not the contrast between the mortal body which even men can kill, and the 'immortal soul' which men cannot touch; it is the contrast between the mere death of the body, the earthly death, and the eternal destruction to which God can deliver

[6] In addition to the literature cited in Note 2, above, see also in reference to Pauline anthropology: W. Gutbrod, *Die paulinische Anthropologie* (Stuttgart, 1934); K. Th. Schäfer, "Der Mensch in paulinischer Auffassung," in *Das Bild vom Menschen* (Düsseldorf, 1934), 25–35; H. Mehl-Koehnlein, *L'homme selon l'Apôtre Paul* (Neuchâtel-Paris, 1951); R. Bultmann, *Theology of the New Testament* (New York, 1962–63); W. D. Stacey, *The Pauline View of Man* (London, 1956); B. Rey, "L'homme nouveau d'après s. Paul," *Revue des Sciences Philosophiques et Théologiques* 48 (1964), 603–629; 49 (1965), 161–195.

man, the whole man."[7] Jesus' words presuppose man's resurrection for the Judgment, "man's bodily presence before the judge, after a more or less disembodied interim state of the soul (10:28a). Only body and soul together constitute the fully responsible human being."[8] Judaism, while giving thought to this "interim state" which follows the death of the body and implies a separation of "body" and "soul," has held fast to the unity of "body and soul." That "interim state" is overcome in the resurrection which alone represents the true and ultimate goal of human existence.[9] The conviction behind the words of Jesus is this, that man is called to share in God's eternal life.

The same thought is expressed paradoxically in these words: "For whoever would save his life will lose it, and whoever loses his life for my sake will find it" (Mt 16:25). This means: whoever wants to assure his own existence in a self-seeking way will lose its true meaning and goal, for human existence

---

[7] J. Schmid, *Das Evangelium nach Matthäus* (Regensburg, 1956), 182 f.

[8] G. Dautezenberg, *loc. cit.*, 149.

[9] With the rise of the belief in the resurrection of the dead and in pondering the "state between," Jewish anthropology also underwent some changes, partly under Hellenistic influences; but it did not abandon the unitary vision of the Bible. Cf. R. Meyer, *Hellenistisches in der rabbinischen Anthropoligie* (Stuttgart, 1937); K. Schubert, "Die Entwicklung der Auferstehungslehre von der nachexilischen bis zur frührabbinischen Zeit," *BZ* 6 (1962), 177–214.

has a deeper dimension which we can reach only
in God. "After the present and the future which
will end some day, there is a future that is definitive."[10] The same thought is expressed in the
well-known words: "For what does it profit a
man, to gain the whole world and forfeit his life?"
(Mk 8:36); and the parable of the rich fool (Lk
12:16–21) seems as if made to illustrate the point.
Though man be firmly bound to this earth, though
his presence in body be part of him, yet in his
true destination he transcends earthly, material
reality. His "human" life is different in kind, and
is more, than any other life to be found on earth,
as Matthew 6:25 makes clear: "Is not life more
than food, and the body more than clothing?" Here
our familiar distinction between "soul" and "body"
fails; each of the parallel lines does in fact mean
all of man in his personal dignity and God-given
destiny. Man's "soul," which is to say his proper
life, is not determined by food alone, however
much it may depend on food; and his "body,"
which is to say his bodily existence, has a higher
vocation than anxiousness about external things,
however much the body with its needs may be
part of human existence on earth.[11] Thus is it quite
consistent for Jesus to defend the resurrection of
the body against the Sadducees (Mk 12:18–27).
Man, such as Jesus sees him, cannot find his ulti-

10 G. Dautzenberg, *loc. cit.,* 58.
11 Gen 17:1; 24:40; 48:15; I Sam 2:35; 2 Kings 20:3;
Is 38:3; Mal 2:6; Ps 56:14.

mate fulfillment on this earth and in this eon; his life is fulfilled only when he, the whole man with all his bodily being, achieves full participation in the life of God.

This integral view of man in the Bible is so important because it does away completely with the danger of our downgrading and despising the body; because it sees man on earth with all his bonds to the physical, animal, and mental areas of existence, and yet upholds the primacy of his spiritual-personal dignity which makes him the image of God, even God's partner, who is called to share in the divine life. This is how man in the Bible stands before God's face, and speaks to God as the great "Thou" which is absolutely superior to man and yet open to man and turned toward him; and thus man finds his real "I" with all the heights and depths of his humanity. And only in this way does man become capable of integrating the lower areas of existence, to which he is bound by his bodily condition, with his higher spiritual-personal being, and of fixing his eyes on the transcendent goal of his human nature.

Man's orientation toward God has as a consequence that he "walks before the Lord" (Gen 17:1; 24:40; 48:15; I Sam 2:35; 2 Kings 20:3; Is 38:3 Mal 2:6; Psalm 56:14). Man is thereby placed under a moral responsibility more firmly than a purely natural ethics could ever do it. God says to Abraham "I am God Almighty; walk before me, and be blameless" (Gen 17:1). The man who would have God's protection and blessing, his presence and friendship, must be "perfect" before him. This "perfection," too, in the sense in which the Bible uses the term,[12] is determined by the Hebraic concept of integral man. That man is "perfect" who realizes in himself the original image of man such as God willed it. The aim is not to develop a "harmonious personality" or to achieve ideal virtue, but to become a man who corresponds to God's image, who faithfully does God's will. In Ecclesiasticus we read: "Their ways are always before him; they are not hidden from his eyes. . . . All their works are as the sun in the sight of God: and his eyes are continually upon their ways" (17:13, 16). Man cannot "hide" from God, any more than could Adam and Eve, and can no more escape from God's calling him to account than Cain could. Man is not thereby subject to a law that is alien to his nature, but rather bound to an order which corresponds to his natural disposition and destiny and leads him to salvation. God's command touches him as a personal summons and inescapable duty, but it also carries the promise of personal salvation.

[12] Cf. F. Nötscher, *Gotteswege und Menschenwege in der Bibel und in Qumran* (Bonn, 1958), 51, 80, 84 ff.; R. Schnackenburg, "Die Vollkommenheit des Christen nach den Evangelien," *Geist und Leben* 32 (1959), 420–433; P. J. Du Plessis, *Teleios. The Idea of Perfection in the New Testament* (Kampen, 1959); see also Part IV below.

THE BOND WITH THE COMMUNITY

Part of the biblical view of man is that the individual is bound to a community, especially to those "natural" communities of family, kin, and nation. Man exists only as a member of the kinship and national group and shares in its life for good or ill; indeed he participates in the guilt and the destiny of the community into which he is born. This sense of solidarity is much more pronounced in Israel, and in the East generally, than it is in the West.[13] Though modern society, with its new and more superficial structures, has pushed those ancient, natural communities into the background, yet the "social" bond (in the widest sense) remains of paramount importance for the realization of true humanity. The Bible further heightens this natural human disposition by looking upon man as "before the face of God." Disastrous collective pride, the power greed of a majority, the arrogance of large nations, they all must come to naught before the Lord, Master of the world. "Behold, the nations are like a drop from a bucket, and are accounted as the dust on the scales. . . . All the nations are as nothing before him, they are accounted by him as less than nothing and emptiness" (Is 40:15–17). All of Israel's greatness consists in this, that God

[13] Cf. J. Pedersen, *Israel. Its Life and Culture* I–II (Copenhagen, 1946), 46–60, 263–279; J. Scharbert, *Solidarität in Segen und Fluch im Alten Testament und in seiner Umwelt* (Bonn, 1958), 1–23; J. De Fraine, *Adam und seine Nachkommen* (Cologne, 1962).

has chosen it in his sovereign will and made it his own people and ally. "The Lord your God has chosen you to be a people for his own possession, out of all the peoples that are on the face of the earth. It was not because you were more in number than any other people that the Lord set his love upon you and chose you, for you were the fewest of all peoples; but it is because the Lord loves you, and is keeping the oath which he swore to your fathers" (Deut 7:6 ff.). This awareness, that the national and political life, too, take place in the face of God, is a fact whose importance cannot be overestimated.

In the New Testament, this natural bond of the individual with his community, and the duty every man has to his "brother," is transcended by the bond among Jesus' disciples and by the new community which Jesus has established with his blood. Jesus breaks through the boundaries of national and religious membership, and opens the way for God's eschatological call addressed to all nations (cf. Mk 14:24; Mt 28:19). At the core of his message is the fundamental equality of all men before God, and their loving devotion to their "neighbors" and even their enemies (Mt 5:44–48) which God commands. By making love of neighbor the greatest of the commandments, Jesus has joined the duty of "social" consciousness and practice inseparably to the love of God.[14]

Paul clearly saw the consequences of this new

[14] Cf. R. Schnackenburg, *The Moral Teaching of the New Testament* (New York, 1965).

bond for the image of man. The new community in Christ has for him become a reality founded in divine grace through baptism. On a higher level, "in Christ," there now "is neither Jew nor Greek, there is neither slave nor free, there is neither male nor female; for you are all one in Christ Jesus" (Gal 3:28). His Letter to the Colossians (3:9) shows clearly that Paul sees emerging here a new image of man which must be realized by moral effort as well: "You have[15] put off the old nature with its practices, and have put on the new nature, which is being renewed in knowledge after the image of its creator. Here there cannot be Greek and Jew, circumcised and uncircumcised, barbarian, Scythian, slave, free man, but Christ is all and in all. Put on then, as God's chosen ones, holy and beloved, compassion. . . ." The apostle here refers explicitly to the creation of man "after the image of God," sees it as becoming a reality again in Christian baptism, and after baptism in the moral striving of the Christians. With complete assurance, Paul includes Christ in this line of thought. In 1 Corinthians 15:47 ff., Christ is seen

---

[15] The participle may also be read as an imperative, continuing the exhortation; e.g. M. Dibelius and H. Greeven, *An die Kolosser, Epheser, an Philemon* (Tübingen, 1953). More probably the participle aorist suggests a backward glance at the event of baptism, cf. Ch. Masson, *L'Epître de s. Paul aux Colossiens* (Comm. du NT X) (Neuchâtel-Paris, 1950), 143, note 6; J. Jervell, *loc. cit.*, 235 f.

as the antitype of the first Adam, the "man from the earth"; Christ is (since the Resurrection) the "man from heaven" to whom we are bound in order to "be conformed to his image" (cf. Rom 8:29). The formation of a "new" man who regains and surpasses the glory in which he was created —a man "conformed to Christ"—is of course a process that will reach completion and achieve its manifest and perfect realization only when the Lord returns "who will change our lowly body to be like his glorious body" (Phil 3:21). But this new eschatological creation begins even in baptism,[16] and expresses itself even in the Christian's life on earth,[17] when he becomes Christ-like and shares in Christ's death in order to live with Christ. It also calls us to moral regeneration in keeping with the divine powers made available to us.[18] The "new man," created in Christ after God's image, is the fulfillment of the divine thought which created man. The "new man" shines forth again in his original glory and moral immaculateness, but also must show his human nature by fellowship and brotherly love for his neighbors—the "love which binds everything together in perfect harmony" (Col 3:14).

[16] Cf. Rom 6:6–11; Col 2:12; 3:1–4; Gal 6:15; 2 Cor 5:17.
[17] Cf. Phil 3:10 f.; 2 Cor 4:10 f.; 13:4.
[18] Cf. Rom 6:4, 12–14; Col 3:5–14; Eph 2:10; 4:20–24; Cf. also J. Jervell, *loc. cit.*, 231–256; B. Rey (see note 6) has developed the idea of the "new man" very well.

But we have run ahead of ourselves; the integral, unitary character of Paul's vision made it unavoidable. We must return now to two different aspects of the biblical image of man, to clarify them further.

THE HISTORICITY OF MAN

The Bible sees man always in his concrete existence which accomplishes itself in history. The Bible does not philosophize about "man as such," or about what sets him apart from animals, and takes hardly any interest at all in the unchanging characteristics of human nature; the Bible is concerned with man's capacities and possibilities for action, and with the means and directives that are to guide his behavior and his decisions. The point will become clearer, perhaps, if we examine once more the idea of "soul" (*nephesh*—ψυχή). The ancient report of Yahweh's creation applies the term indifferently to man and animals (cf. Gen 2:7 and 2:19). The point of difference between man and beast which this report notes as essential is expressed in a different manner: God, after he had "out of the ground formed every beast of the field and every bird of the air," brought them to Adam "to see what he would call them; and whatever the man called every living creature, that was its name" (Gen 2:19). In this act of name-giving, man not only shows his superiority and dominance over the animal kingdom, but performs also a "creative" and ordering activity. "Here, then, an

act of emulative creation is performed in this name-
giving, and an act of ordering and appropriation
by which man takes mental possession of the creatures."[19] Man shares with the animals an existence
on earth, but by his mental and spiritual capacities
he raises it to a special, precisely a "human" existence. By means of this creative mental activity,
man intervenes in the flow of earthly events and
launches "history." In this activity he experiences
himself as an "historical" being. But the Bible,
viewing man in his historical activity, once again
sees him in his relation to God. The whole process
of historical becoming takes place before God, and
God determines and guides it despite man's freedom of action.

There is at the beginning a fatal act of man,
the "fall from grace." Although this act may be
recounted in the form of a "myth," and although
the account may have originated[20] as a "justification of God" in Israel's retrospective view of history, the ancient tale nonetheless fixes the obscure
origin of all human history. Once again, the state
of "fallen man" is not described in detail, but is
made vivid by the effects of original sin on man's
life and earthly existence: woman's pain in child-

[19] G. von Rad, *Genesis: a Commentary* (Philadelphia, 1961).
[20] Thus N. Lohfink, "Die Erzählung vom Sündenfall," in *Das Siegeslied am Schilfmeer* (Frankfurt, 1965), 81–101; see also H. Renckens, *Israel's Concept of the Beginning* (Mainz, 1959).

bed and man's toil and sweat, the expulsion from the garden, man's subjection to death—and later on, man's fatal behavior, Cain's fratricide and the progressive collapse of morals. The Fall is the real starting point of man's "history," a history of doom into which light and hope are brought only by God's intervention. As he reads of the historical behavior of his forefathers, the Hebrew comes to understand his own nature, to see that "the imagination of man's heart is evil from his youth" (Gen 8:21, cf. 6:5), that "there is no man who does not sin" (1 Kg 8:46), that "both we and our fathers have sinned" (Ps 106:6; cf. Jer 3:25, Dn 9:5 f.); and he comprehends that his own existence is involved in the guilt and the destiny of the whole nation.

Of course, this is a somber view of moral conduct, and a negative judgment on human "history"; but it keeps us from dreaming of a world-embracing humaneness and a paradise on earth where all men will be happy. And yet the Bible is far from pessimistic about man's future. It is just that the Bible does not look for man's salvation to man himself—man who, history shows, has failed a thousand times and will fail again—but to God, or at least to the man who clings to God and obeys him. Man acting in history needs God's counsel and help, his guidance and instruction on "the way of life."[21] What drove Israel again and again toward the divine presence, into the arms of God, was not a generalized faith in God, nor any

[21] Cf. Jer 21:8; Ps 16:11; Prov 4:10–19; 6:23.

18

doctrine of a revelation remote from history, but the historic experience of their own distress and failure, and the historic experience, on the other hand, of divine help, estrangement, punishment, and renewed pity. In their historical existence, indeed here most of all, man and nation stand before God's face and depend on him, because they cannot stand up otherwise, as Isaiah (7:9) says: "If you will not believe, surely you shall not be established." There is light in the future, and man is able to bear the darkness of the present and of his own existence, only through the demonstrations of pity, and through the promises, of God.[22]

In the New Testament, too, when the time of salvation is proclaimed and commences, man is not freed of his historic ties. Jesus proclaims the nearness of the kingdom of God (Mk 1:15), the "acceptable year of the Lord" (Lk 4:19), but by this very proclamation confronts men with the urgent and inescapable decision, either to seize the salvation that is now offered them, or else sink irretrievably into perdition. The hour in which God decides to establish his complete dominion is man's fateful hour (cf. Lk 12:54–56; 17:26–30); the coming of the last bearer of revelation and savior becomes the hour of crisis (cf. Jn 3:18 f.). Jesus knows himself bound to the time fixed for him,[23] and accepts the "hour" of his death as the will of

[22] Cf. Part III, below.
[23] Cf. Lk 13:22 f.; Jn 9:4; 11:9.

the Father.[24] But he also addresses his contemporaries with prophetic urgency,[25] and reproves "this generation" which will not listen to his voice and be converted.[26] The eschatological event does not relieve man of the historic decision—it compels him to make it.[27]

The early church at that juncture—advancing another step along the road toward the goal of history and the divine plan of salvation—took up Jesus' eschatological appeal and passed it on to the faithful. For Jesus is now the exalted Lord who exercised God's dominion in this era tending toward the "end," and wants to realize it through his Church on earth and throughout the universe.[28] The summons of the proclaimers resounds at the precise moment of salvation attained although not yet completed, and it reaches the faithful in their singular situation within the history of salvation. "Behold, now is the acceptable time; behold, now is the day of salvation" (2 Cor 6:2), the time, that is, to render fruitful the God-given grace in the midst of the ongoing present evil age (cf. Gal 1:4; Eph 5:16; 6:12–18). The age moves on, and calls for ever greater watchfulness, composure, and readiness. "You know what hour it is, how it is full

[24] Cf. Mk 14:41; Lk 22:53; Jn 12:27; 13:1; 17:1.
[25] Cf. Lk 13:6–9; 19:41–44; Mk 9–1; 13:30.
[26] Cf. Mt 11:16–19; Mk 8:12; Lk 11, 31 ff.
[27] Cf. R. Schnackenburg, *God's Rule and Kingdom* (New York, 1963).
[28] *Ibid.*

time now for you to wake from sleep. For salvation
is nearer to us now than when we first believed;
the night is far gone, the day is at hand. Let us
then cast off the works of darkness and put on the
armor of light. . . ." (Rom 13:11; cf. 1 Thess
5:6–10). The "eschatological" attitude which Paul
bids the Christian to assume is anything but a
feverish, apocalyptic expectation of the parousia.
Christian existence is, of course, eschatological,
that is, at "the end of the ages" (1 Cor 10:11),
focused upon the coming ages (cf. Eph 2:5 ff.),
and unworldly, with minds not set on earthly
things (cf. Phil 3:19), not conformed to this world
(cf. Rom 12:2; 1 Cor 7:29 ff.); but nonetheless it
is historical, bound to this age and calling on
the Christian to prove himself on earth.[29] His
heightened watchfulness due to this eschatological
perspective allows the Christian consciously to
overcome the present.[30]

Though placing its emphasis differently, Johan-
nine theology teaches the same attitude. In the
gospel of John, the word of God's son come into
the world has an "eschatological," critical power.
Here every man is faced with the decision whether
to believe in the bearer of the revelation and savior
and so to win life, or to remain in unbelief and

[29] Cf. Gal 1:4; Eph 5:16; 6:12–18.
[30] Cf. E. Neuhäusler, *Anspruch und Antwort Gottes*
(Düsseldorf, 1962), 215–234; E. Lövestam, *Spiritual
Wakefulness in the New Testament* (Lund, 1963);
W. Ott, *Gebet und Heil* (Munich, 1965).

under the wrath of God.[31] But those who follow the divine bearer of light and life are not called out of the world, but sent into the world (cf. Jn 17:15–18). These children of God whom the world has chosen remain in the world, and must face it with all its anguish, persecutions, and temptations.[32] True, they are already replete with God's life and God's love and filled with joy and peace; the result, however, is not a world-rejecting mysticism but the commandment to love one's brother, and to express this love by helping and self-sacrificing deeds (1 Jn 3:14–18; 4:19 ff.).

What this message of the New Testament signifies for the image of man is this: man cannot find his deepest joy and highest strength, or consolation from the earth's distress and freedom from inner compulsion, by leaving the setting of his life behind, fleeing the world, or seeking ecstasy; he can find them only in his historical existence, as himself a part of the web of earthly things and events. Just as the history of salvation is not a "superhistory," but history under the aspect of salvation, just so the Christian believer does not become a "superman," an exceptional creature among the rest of mankind; he becomes a whole man in whom

[31] Cf. 3:36; 5:24; 8:12; 12:46 f. See also J. Blank, *Untersuchungen zur johanneischen Christologie und Eschatologie* (Freiburg i. Br., 1964), 73 f., 91–95; R. Schnackenburg, *Das Johannesevangelium* I, (Freiburg i. Br., 1965), 401–404, 426 ff.
[32] Cf. Jn 15:18 ff; 16:33; 1 Jn 2:15 ff.

all dimensions of human nature, including the profoundest and supreme dimensions, are realized. Only when man as he exists on earth and in history binds himself to God, surrenders to him, and is raised up by God and guided toward his goal, only then does he become the true man who achieves freedom and the perfection of his humanity. This view of man implies, of course, that man is regarded not merely as the most highly evolved living being on earth. Seen with the eyes of faith, man is tending toward a goal which transcends his existence on earth and in history. This is the aspect under which we shall now look once more at the biblical image of man.

MAN AND HIS SALVATION

The belief which is fundamental in the Bible is that man finds happiness and salvation in his communion with God, by living in complete union with God. God is the fullness of life and light, and the more man shares in that fullness, the more he fulfills his desire for a life led in light and happiness. This view of human existence of the believer coincides with the secularized view of many people today in expressing the desire that all man's vital forces and vital possibilities may reach their full realization; the two views differ in their interpretation of what constitutes a truly human, fulfilled, and ample life. The man who is centered upon himself and on the world craves the material goods of life; he may wish to acquire also the more refined "spiritual" and cultural values; but he has no desire for the absolute, the fullness of being and value. The religious man, on the other hand, shares St. Augustine's conviction that his heart will never be at peace until it rests in God. Two attitudes toward life are confronted here whose radical difference cannot be denied. The point at issue, however, is which of the two stands up more firmly under the stresses to which life subjects all men, which of the two bears up better under the darkness of human existence. The Bible is exceedingly instructive on this point, since it lets us experience, often in a deeply stirring manner, man's struggle to solve the problems of life, and to win through "before God."

Psalm 30, for example, the song of a man who has been rescued from the brink of death, perhaps from grievous illness, gives us an insight into his thoughts under good and ill fortune. "I said in my prosperity, 'I shall never be moved.' By thy favor, O Lord, thou hadst established me as a strong mountain; thou didst hide thy face, I was dismayed" (Ps 30:6 f.). The singer admits freely that his prosperity had made him secure and careless; now, after the trial, he sees his prosperity as God's gift. For he has learned meanwhile that good fortune and health cannot be taken for granted, and that he, too, is exposed and vulnerable. He has been in grave danger, which he now understands as having been ordained by God; God, as he says, "did hide his face." Then he called on the Lord, and the Lord heard him; and now he sings his

24

song of praise, and will give thanks to God forever. Through this experience, man has not only come closer to God, he has also gained a deeper understanding of his own human condition, he has "matured" as we say; he now leads a more aware life, with a greater knowledge of the heights and depths of human existence. He has gained this insight "before God," and from now on he will turn toward God, dedicate himself to God, more fully. Many of the psalms are expressions of this safe return to God. Psalm 36 formulates with special beauty what this step means to man: "How precious is thy steadfast love, O God! The children of men take refuge in the shadow of thy wings. They feast on the abundance of thy house, and thou givest them drink from the river of thy delights. For with thee is the fountain of life; in thy light do we see light" (Ps 36:7–9).

But the road of the devout does not always lead back into the light; in fact, he will often see godless men faring much better than himself. Psalm 73 lets us share the inner experience of a man struggling with such a situation before God, beginning with a vivid description of the "wicked": "For they have no pangs; their bodies are sound and sleek. They are not in trouble as other men are; they are not stricken like other men. Therefore pride is their necklace; violence covers them as a garment . . ." (vv. 4–6). The temptation of the faithful is that he is singled out to suffer and be troubled. "All in vain I have kept my heart clean and washed my hands in innocence" (v. 13). But then he understands that the happiness of the wicked is only an illusion. "Truly thou dost set them in slippery places; thou dost make them fall to ruin. How they are destroyed in a moment, swept away utterly by terrors!" (v. 18 f.). It has been rightly observed that the "end" (v. 17) of the wicked in this description must be more than mere physical destruction, since its counterpart, describing the bliss of the righteous, does not aim at long life and material welfare. Although his material condition has not changed, the psalmist says: "My flesh and my heart may fail, but God is the strength of my heart and my portion forever" (v. 26). God has become his portion, even though the righteous shares the fate of all men that he must die. Eichrodt[33] expressed the point well when he wrote that the righteous man, with all his trials and tribulations, knows "of a life with God, of being held in God's hand, of being guided by God's counsel, and thus knows that life has a content which our external fortunes cannot affect." Accordingly, the situation of the wicked that has been described must be understood thus, again in Eichrodt's excellent formulation: "What makes their situation, outwardly so secure, a slippery place where men enmeshed in insubstantial illusions are forever threatened with that dreadful fall, is that God will give them not another thought when their hour of death arrives but dismisses

[33] W. Eichrodt, *Theology of the Old Testament* (Philadelphia, 1961–67).

them like an empty dream, so that they then are indeed faced with the horror of nothingness."[34] The view the Bible takes of man's salvation or perdition here stands revealed: the decision lies in man's relation to God. Even material happiness on earth remains an illusion if man does not attain the ultimate profundity of human existence; while on the other hand even a man who lives in misery and sorrow can still give meaning and content to his life before God.

The psalm is so remarkable because the psalmist obviously has no knowledge as yet of eternal life with God, or of retribution after death. We know that the idea of resurrection emerged only comparatively late in biblical revelation, and that life after death in *Sheol* (the realm of the dead) was conceived only as a shadowy existence, like a diminished earthly life and without life's full-blooded freshness.[35] Here is expressed some of the reticence of the earliest revelation, which God intended to carry only gradually to its fullest clarity, and to completion only in the New Testament. Thus Psalm 73 unintentionally renders us a great service. The frequently heard objection, that the believer consoles himself with a reward in the

[34] *Ibid.*
[35] Cf. P. Heinisch, *Theologie des Alten Testamentes* (Bonn, 1940), 244–249; R. Tournay, "L'eschatologie individuelle dans les Psaumes," in *Revue Biblique* 56 (1949), 481–506; P. Van Imschoot, *loc. cit.*, 45–63; K. Schubert, *loc. cit.* (Note 9).

beyond, cannot apply here; here the believer does not look into a misty distance to find the happiness he did not find on earth, does not dream of a heavenly paradise and close his eyes to his own inability to improve conditions here on earth. What we are dealing with here, on the contrary, is the victory over the earth's darkness by an inner light that breaks forth from the communion with God and from the vital current which comes from that communion. This is the inner conquest of mortal man's desperate situation, and the removal of the limitations to his humanity which beset man on earth. And so we read in Psalm 16: "Therefore my heart is glad, and my soul rejoices; my body also dwells secure. For thou dost not give me up to Sheol, or let thy godly one see the Pit. Thou dost show me the path of life; in thy presence there is fullness of joy, in thy right hand are pleasures for evermore" (16:9–11). While we are not yet free to read into this passage a belief in the continued life of the "soul" with God, nor the concealed idea of the resurrection, we do see that fear of death is overcome by the certainty that man is always "in the face of God." Many of the more recent commentators take the view that this psalm (as well as Psalm 49:16) does nonetheless betray the hope of a communion with God which even death does not terminate, even though the psalmist did not know how this could be, nor even raise the question; so that these passages would after all show a dawning premonition of what only later revelation would clearly disclose.[36]

It remains true, of course, that man's complete salvation requires that he share in God's eternal life. We encounter this belief among the Hellenistic Jews in their hope of immortality,[37] and among many Jews in the certainty of resurrection. Christ confirmed this belief, and offered scriptural proof to the Sadducees who did not share it (Mk 12:24–27).[38] This doctrine had long caused difficulties, and scandal, to Greek and Gnostic thought (cf. Acts 17:32; 1 Cor 15). Today, with modern philosophy increasingly rejecting a dualism of body and soul, the idea of the soul's immortality may well encounter as much resistance as the idea of the resurrection of the body. But

[36] Cf. R. Kittel, *Die Psalmen* (Leipzig, 1929), 51 ff.; A. Weiser, *The Psalms, a Commentary* (Göttingen, 1959), 119; W. Eichrodt, *loc. cit.*, 367. The following differ: H. Gunkel, *Die Psalmen* (Göttingen, 1926), 51; R. Tournay, *loc. cit.*, 490–493; H. J. Kraus, *Psalmen* I (Neukirchen, 1960), 125 f., who speaks, however, of a "mysterious transparence," p. 127.

[37] Especially in Proverbs; cf. 3:1–4; 5:15 f.

[38] On Jesus' interpretation, which goes beyond the literal meaning of Ex 3:6, cf. F. Dreyfus, "L'argument scriptuaire de Jésus en faveur de la résurrection des morts (Marc, XII, 26–27)," *Revue Biblique* 66 (1959), 213–224: God always proves himself as the protector and savior, the "God of the living," ultimately also at the resurrection.

the old question is still with us: How does man
achieve the true fulfillment of his human nature,
his "authenticity," his inner freedom, his full
human dignity (or whatever we may call it)? The
New Testament speaks of salvation, of man being
saved (δωιηρία), or of "eternal life" (ζωὴ αἰώνιος),
and refers most often to the eschatological perfection in God's kingdom to come; it thus presupposes the resurrection, yet without denying that
in the interim man will live with God. The alternative "Immortality of the soul, or resurrection of the dead?" is without justification in this
sharp formulation[39] if our question concerns the
ultimate fulfillment of Christian existence.[40] It is

[39] O. Cullmann, *Immortality of the Soul or Resurrection of the Dead?* (New York, 1958), proposes to
eliminate completely the idea of immortality in the
New Testament. No doubt that idea in its Platonic
form can hardly be found in the New Testament; but
that does not exclude a continued life after death,
a more Semitic idea of a state between (cf. Lk
16:19–31; 23:43). See the discussion in *New Testament Abstracts* 2 (1957/58), 84; also J. Gnilka, "Die
biblische Jenseitserwartung: Unsterblichkeitshoff-
nung-Auferstehungsglaube?" *Bibel und Leben* 5
(1964), 103–116.

[40] For Paul who, in keeping with his Semitic manner of
thinking, expects primarily the bodily resurrection
at the parousia (which he hopes for presently) the
difficulty that he might die before it is solved by his
union with Christ. He comforts himself with the
thought that then (as at the parousia, cf. 1 Thess

of course the indefeasible conviction of the entire New Testament[41] that life on earth does not exhaust and fulfill man's existence. All who believe in Christ see the proof of this conviction not only in the words of Jesus on earth, but most of all in the resurrection of the Crucified by God "who gives life to the dead and calls into existence the things that do not exist" (Rom 4:17).

Man today is in the gravest danger of "losing himself," in every sense of the expression: "losing

4:17) he will be with Christ (δὺν Χριδτῷ) (cf. Phil. 1:23), or will be "away from the body and at home with the Lord" (πρὸς τὸν κύριον) (2 Cor 5:8). The passage 2 Cor 5:1–10 is exegetically much in dispute. In addition to the Commentaries, see J. N. Sevenster in *New Testament Studies* 1 (1954/55), 291–296; A. Feuillet, "La demeure céleste et la destinée des chrétiens," *Recherches de Science Religieuse* 44 (1956), 161–192, 360–402; S. Garofalo, "Sulla 'escatologia intermedia' in S. Paolo," *Gregorianum* 39 (1958), 335–352; E. E. Ellis, "II Cor V, 1–10 in Pauline Eschatology," *New Testament Studies* 6 (1959/60), 211–224; G. Wagner, "Le tabernacle et la vie 'en Christ,'" *Revue d'Histoire et de Philosophie Religieuse* 41 (1961), 379–393; P. Hoffmann, *Die Toten in Christus* (Münster, 1966), esp. 253–285 (the verse does not relate to the state between).

[41] The thought varies in form according to the theological views and eschatological attitude of the authors. On Paul, see the essay "Between the Times," on John the essay "Life and Death According to John," in the sequel to this work, Part II.

31

himself" in his business and his diversions, "losing himself" in the anonymity of the mass, and finally in the true sense "losing his own *self*." How can he "find himself again"? Only if he, like the man of the Bible, stands "before God" and clings to God, to God the Father "through whom are all things and through whom we exist" (1 Cor 8:6)— only if, having died with Christ, he walks with him in newness of life and is united with him in a resurrection like his (Rom 6:4–5).

II

The Penitential Sermon in the New Testament

The call for "conversion" or "penitence" (Greek μειάνοια) is present throughout the New Testament. Modern man, open to the world and glad to be alive, is not very receptive to such a summons. The word "penitence" brings to his mind practices of abstinence and self-denial, and characters like John the Baptist, monks, and ascetics who seem to him out of harmony with today's age of technology and physical culture, travel, and sports. It may be that right after the fearful disaster of World War I, we were more susceptible to such a call to change our ways;[1] but today we have built a new and more beautiful world from the ruins of the old, and are more afflu-

---

[1] The present essay was first given as a paper at a theologians' meeting in 1948, and was published in 1950 in *Münchner Theologische Zeitschrift* (Vol. 1, No. 4) under the title "Typen der Metanoia-Predigt im Neuen Testament." The present text has been extensively revised.

ent than ever. But it would mean to mistake the New Testament's call for penitence if we were to limit it to renunciation and penance, if we were to restrict it to the superficial aspects of the material life. The message of the New Testament concerns man in the depth of his human existence. It demands from him a fundamental decision on how he will act toward the world and toward his fellow men, how he will understand himself, and how he will seek his salvation. "Conversion" is the fundamental, all-embracing command which places all men before God and summons them to respond to the evangel of Christ, God's message of salvation at the appointed hour. This call, which Christ himself has raised, has a bright and joyful ring, quite different from our gloomy word "penitence"; because we are called to revert to God, with whom there is joy over every returning sinner, who has prepared a joyous banquet for him and gives him of the fullness of his joy (Lk 15:7, 10, 20–24).

It is instructive to study what view the synoptic gospels take of Jesus' message of conversion, against the background of the prophetic sermons of conversion up to John the Baptist, and how the early Church takes this message, transmutes it, and applies it to the conditions of its time. Each of the theologians of the early Church has understood the call for conversion in his own way, and interpreted it for his audience accordingly. But let us first take a quick look at the concept itself, since it sounds different from the Hebrew even in Greek, and in our modern languages could easily lead to misunderstandings.

In secular Greek usage, the term "metanoia" means "change of mind," or the "repentance" of past deeds. But today scholars are agreed[2] that the concept of the New Testament is not identical with the Greek meaning of the word, nor with classical-Hellenistic usage, but harks back rather to the usage of the Old Testament and the Jews, which is based on certain ideas and traditions. Again, the concept has to be distinguished from preprophetic ideas. It does not mean the erasure of ritual or moral mistakes, or restitution for an injustice com-

[2] Recent literature: A. H. Dirksen, *The New Testament Concept of Metanoia* (Washington, 1932); E. K. Dietrich, *Die Umkehr (Bekehrung und Busse) im Alten Testament und Judentum* (Stuttgart, 1936); O. Michel, "Die Umkehr nach der Verkündung Jesu," *Evangelische Theologie* 5 (1938), 403–413; H. Pohlmann, *Die Metanoia als Zentralbegriff der christlichen Frömmigkeit* (Leipzig, 1938); J. Behm, in *ThWNT* IV, 972–1004; J. Gewiess, "Metanoia im Neuen Testament," *Die Kirche in der Welt* II (Münster, 1948), 149–152; H. Braun, " 'Umkehr' in spätjüdisch-häretischer und frühchristlicher Sicht," *Zeitschrift für Theologie und Kirche* 50 (1953), 243–258; H. Braun, *Spätjüdisch-häretischer und frühchristlicher Radikalismus*, 2 vols. (Tübingen, 1957); W. L. Holladay, *The Root šûbh in the Old Testament* (Leiden, 1958); *La Conversion* (various contributions) in *Lumière et Vie* 47 (1960); P. Aubin, Le problème de la Conversion (Paris, 1963); W. Trilling, "Metanoia als Grundforderung der neutestamentlichen Lebenslehre," in *Einübung des Glaubens* (*Festschrift für Klemens Tilmann*) (Würzburg, 1965), 178–190.

mitted ("penance"), but, after the Hebrew *shûb* (Aramaic *tûb*), it means return. In the Old Testament this is an action word, and by this token alone serves notice that what is required is an active conduct. What underlies it is the image of the road: we turn back from the wrong direction, and take a new road. Only the rabbinist tradition developed it into a firmly defined theological concept; the substantive *teshubah* (Aramaic *tetuba*) becomes the expression of certain views typical of Judaism obedient to the law. Jesus himself still uses the word entirely in the sense of the prophets.

This gives us the proper starting point for an understanding of the concept as used in the New Testament. It means total reversal, a remaking of man's very essence. Conversion does not remain an inner attitude, but presses outward to express itself in action. Man from now on knows only one single goal: God; he hears God's call and answers it with unlimited willingness.

In this way, conversion becomes man's essential answer to Jesus' message that the kingdom of God is at hand (Mk 1:15). And being thus most intimately tied to the proclamation of God's kingdom, conversion also assumes a special character in keeping with the particular form of the proclamation, in keeping with the given hour of salvation history. If the coming of Christ is the "fullness of time," then the immediate "precursor" (John the Baptist), the "Now" (the fulfillment of time in Jesus Christ), and the "time of the Church" between Christ's assumption and parousia must each give its specific stamp to the call for conversion. The given situation in the history of salvation influences the form in which the call for conversion is raised.[3] The personality of the proclaimer, the nature of the audience, the setting and the conditions of the time also have their influence. Thus there arise even in the New Testament diverse forms of the call for conversion, through all of which we must hear the unchanging demand of God. Our task now is to achieve an understanding of the call for conversion that is in keeping with the present hour—which is still the hour of salvation—and in keeping with our present spiritual condition; and then to let it enter our hearts.

JOHN THE BAPTIST AND HIS CALL FOR CONVERSION

The great forerunner of the Messiah initially continues in the line of the Old Testament prophets with his call for conversion. Just as the prophets criticized externalized cultic religion and called for a profound, active, and effective return to Yahveh, just so John the Baptist stresses the need for turning back to God in a genuine fashion, without sham. He hurls violent threats at those allegedly righteous men, especially the scribes and Pharisees, who do not feel any need for conversion in

[3] On the changes in the concept of God's kingdom in the history of revelation and of salvation, see R. Schnackenburg, *God's Rule and Kingdom* (New York, 1963).

their hearts, even though they do not dissociate themselves from the popular movement around the baptist at the Jordan. They regard themselves as sons of Abraham by virtue of descent and their obedience to the law, and thus assured of God's messianic promises of grace. But the shaggy preacher of penitence calls out to them, just as the prophets of old called out to the temple-goers and givers of sacrifices who acted from mere habit, without inner involvement, and summons them to moral conversion: "Bear fruit that befits repentance!" (Mt 3:8). John is as certain of the imminence of divine wrath and judgment as were the ancient preachers of doom and punishment. Like Amos and Hosea, he regards the catastrophe as inevitable; only those willing to be converted can escape the judgment. The Messiah is ready, winnowing fork in hand, to clear his threshing floor. He will burn the chaff in unquenchable fire; only the wheat will be gathered into the granary (Mt 3:12).

But with all the similarities between John's sermons of conversation and those of the prophets, there is one decisive point in which he goes beyond them. What he announces is not just some divine judgment, but the final judgment day at the end of time, enacted by God through his Messiah. While the prophets point to current dangers, to lend color to their predictions of disaster and urgency to their call for repentance, the preacher at the Jordan announces the imminent appearance of the Messiah who will burn a corrupt world in the fire of judgment. All those who hear his voice are here given their one, last opportunity to return to God.

In Matthew, the baptist's message is exactly the same as that of Christ himself: "Repent, for the kingdom of heaven is at hand!" (Mt 3:2; 4:17). But even though the forerunner raises the same cry as he whom he announces, we must not fail to hear the special note which distinguished it from the words of Jesus.[4] When he speaks of him who is to come (Mt 11:3), he is thinking of the executor of divine judgment, and not so much of him through whom God's mercy and love are made visible. He expects the kingdom of God to arrive in a storm of violence, in the immediate future, with the Messiah's first appearance. This vision gives his summons to conversion its urgent, compelling tone, and also that somber earnestness, increased still further by the appearance of renunciation and flight from the world which he presents in his own person. From what we know of his preachments, he seems transfixed by the vision of the judgment, and finds nothing to say about the salvation which the Messiah will bring. The axe is already laid to the root; every tree that does not bear good fruit will be cut down and thrown into the fire (Mt 3:10; Lk 3:9). According to Luke 3:10–14, fully in keeping with the radical social concern of the third

---

[4] Cf. Schnackenburg, *ibid.*, W. Trilling, "Die Täufertradition bei Matthäus" in *BZ* 3 (1959), 278–289, esp. 285 ff.

evangelist, the baptist makes concrete demands: "He who has two coats, let him share with him who has none; and he who has food, let him do likewise" (Lk 3:11). With the thunderclouds of the Messiah's imminent judgment hanging over them, all men must divest themselves of their earthly belongings, because—and this is the meaning of his call—the divine judge and his executor recognize no class nor rank, and insist on action, not mere words. On the other hand nobody, not even the ill-famed publicans and mercenaries, is incapable of escaping the divine punishment by conversion.

Such penitential sermons—for that is what John's preaching is—are time-bound, of course, but even so they show us the necessarily radical nature of a true conversion. John merely stands in the doorway which leads from the Old Testament to the New, he is not yet a spokesman of the message of mercy which Christ will bring.[5] But his

[5] The baptist's inquiry from prison, whether Jesus was "he who is to come," would be prompted by his astonishment at the manner of Jesus' conduct. The image of the messiah which John saw in his own mind, and which he presented to the people, had nothing in common with Jesus' peaceful behavior— Jesus spoke only of the mercy, not the wrath of God; cf. Lk 4:19, where the quotation from Is 61:2 stops after the "acceptable year of the Lord," and says nothing of "the day of vengeance of our God." John's prophetic mission shared his human limitations and his thinking habits in terms of the Jewish Old Testa-

prophetic call assumes significance wherever God's
offer of mercy is mistaken for a sign of weakness,
and where Christ's proclamation of salvation is rejected (cf. Mt 11:16–19), for there the gospel itself
becomes the judgment (Lk 10:10–12; Jn 3:16–18).
John's call for conversion is impressively and effec-
tively supported by the baptism in the river Jordan, which Mark 1:4 and Luke 3:3 call "a baptism
of repentance for the forgiveness of sins." Mark
1:6 (and likewise Matthew 3:6) describe to us the
event, in which those to be baptized confessed
their sins while descending into the river. This
baptism is not a rite of atonement similar to the
customary ritual ablutions and submersions of
Judaism; for while those could be repeated, John's

ment. He stood at the turning point from the Old
to the New Testament; and this fact is reflected in
the way in which the early Church judged him. In
Matthew and Luke, citing source Q, he is called
"more than a prophet," he is the promised messenger
and preparer of the Messiah's way, among those
born of women none is greater than he (Mt 11:9 ff.,
Lk 7, 26 ff.). Luke counts him to the period of the
law and the prophets (16:16); cf. H. Conzelmann,
The Theology of St. Luke (New York, 1960). Mark
includes him, as the man who fulfilled Elias' proph-
ecies, in the period of salvation that begins with
Jesus; cf. J. M. Robinson, *The Problem of History
in Mark* (London, 1957); in John's Gospel he is
Jesus' immediate witness, although he is not—for
reasons other than those of Luke—the promised Elias
(cf. Jn 1:19–34; 3:28–30; 5:33–35).

baptism takes place one time only. It is to give men the capacity to enter now, at this moment at the end of time, into God's community of the saved. The fact that baptism, according to Matthew 3:11, is given by John "for repentance"—that is, with conversion its meaning and its purpose, means more precisely: Man's will to repent is manifested in this baptism, and at the same time so confirmed by baptism that it becomes a fully effective return to God, assured of God's mercy. Here the profundity of the idea is revealed: Conversion is not a human deed easily performed, a human attitude easily assumed, but a total transformation of man's inmost nature, so radical that it needs the assistance of God's grace. To render that assistance is one of the purposes of John's baptism.[6]

[6] It is a matter of controversy whether John ascribed to his baptism merely symbolic significance or a sacramental effect. However, John's baptism was surely more than a mere symbol; it was the admission, through God, to the number of those who would escape the impending day of wrath, a kind of support and aid from God to those who were willing to repent. Cf. W. F. Flemington, *The New Testament Doctrine of Baptism* (London, 1948), 13–23 (page 22: "extension of the symbolic acts of the prophets" which were "not purely representative but also in some way effective"); C. H. Kraeling, *John the Baptist* (New York-London, 1951), 95–122 (symbolic act of voluntary submission to God's judgment); G. R. Beasley-Murray, *Baptism in the New Testament* (London, 1962), 31–44 (combination of

CHRIST'S CALL FOR CONVERSION

Christ's call for conversion goes far beyond that of John, for he proclaims: *"The time is fulfilled, and the kingdom of God is at hand; repent, and believe in the gospel!"* (Mk 1:15). The call thus shifts from the time of imminent expectation to the time of fulfillment. Christ demands conversion as the fundamental condition for admission into the kingdom of God with its riches. Or better: Conversion is man's answer to God's great offer of salvation. And man is to give this answer as spontaneously and generously as does, for example, the chief tax collector Zaccheaeus, who is so overpowered by Christ's visit to his house that he is willing to give half of his possessions to the poor (Lk 19:5–8). This house had found salvation; God's call had been answered.

Therefore it is culpable beyond understanding if men do not listen to Jesus' call for conversion. "The men of Nineveh will arise at the judgment with this generation and condemn it; for they repented at the preaching of Jonah, and behold, something greater than Jonah is here" (Mt 12:41; Lk 11:32). And that here is indeed "something greater than Jonah," that God's royal power and the working of divine grace are coming forward

human and divine action); J. Gnilka, "Der Täufer Johannes und der Ursprung der christlichen Taufe," in *Bibel und Leben* 4 (1963), 39–49 (page 46: no "sacramental" effect, but the announcement of forgiveness of sins by God).

through Jesus, everyone can recognize by the deeds of Divine power worked by Jesus. Those who do not convert despite this evidence are therefore inexcusable. This is the meaning of that cry of woe which Jesus raises over the towns of Galilee that had seen most of his mighty works. "Woe to you Chorazin! woe to you, Bethsaida! for if the mighty works done in you had been done in Tyre and Sidon, they would have repented long ago in sackcloth and ashes. But I tell you, it shall be more tolerable on the day of judgment for Tyre and Sidon than for you" (Mt 11:21; Lk 10:13 f.).

The conversion call from the lips of God's last emissary, the lips of him who indeed now proclaims the expected kingdom of God, is addressed to *all men.* It is addressed to everyone, because everyone is a sinner before the Lord. Jesus' messengers, too, when they are first sent out, are to raise the call for conversion; that call contains everything that God expects from man in the hour of salvation (Mk 6:12). Jesus' pronouncement on the need for conversion is given its cutting edge by his repeated attacks on the hypocrites and the self-righteous. The crude, notorious sinners acknowledge their sin and guilt before God, and turn back to God in honest contrition, relying on nothing, trusting in nothing but God's mercy—and this is why there will be more joy in heaven, with God, over one sinner who repents than over ninety-nine righteous men (Lk 15:7–10). Jesus sketches the two contrasting attitudes in the parable of the Pharisee and the pub-

lican, in a portrait of supreme mastery done with
few but telling lines (Lk 18:10–14). The contrite
publican bowed down by the consciousness of
his guilt, but nonetheless trustingly imploring
God's forgiveness, personifies what Jesus means
by conversion. In the parable of the lost son (Lk
15:11–32), the action of the younger son who
leaves his father's house and in the far country
falls into want illustrates the essence of conversion: the coming to himself, the return, the home-
coming. Luke 13:1 shows with special clarity Jesus'
opposition to the then customary standards of sin
and punishment, guilt and expiation. (Lk 13:1 ff.).
When he learns of the massacre of Galileans at the
sacrifices,[7] he raises his voice against the tacit
assumption that they had met their death at a
sacred place because of their exceptionally serious
sins. "Do you think that these Galileans were
worse sinners than all the other Galileans, because
they suffered thus? I tell you, No; but unless you
repent you will all likewise perish" (Lk 13:2–4).
In Jesus' eyes all men are sinners deserving punishment, but what arouses him is that they will
not understand this, and think themselves holier
than their fellows. Men must overcome this wrong-
headedness, and uproot the last remaining traces
of self-righteousness in their hearts. Only the total
surrender of human pride is the return to God.

[7] Cf. J. Blinzler, "Die Niedermetzelung von Galiläern
durch Pilatus," in *Novum Testamentum* 2 (1957),
24–49.

Jesus also gives us a positive illustration of complete self-surrender and submission to God when he uses the image of the child. "Truly, I say to you, whoever does not receive the kingdom of God like a child shall not enter it" (Lk 10:15). The attitude of the man who returns to God consists in this, that before God he is like a child.[8]

We have gained a deeper insight into the *essence* of that conversion which Jesus calls for. We cannot limit it to the repentance of sins committed (as though Jesus had spoken only of the repentant sinner). Nor can we limit it to penitential practices intended to reconcile a wrathful God (as though Jesus had spoken only of sackcloth and ashes). These words of Jesus highlight only partial aspects of conversion. Jesus does not demand fasting (Mk 2:19), but he does demand conversion. Conversion is man's total attitude in the face of God, a new self-understanding before the holy and yet kind and merciful God. And that attitude implies the resolute rejection of all that is sinful and averse to God, all that is human self-seeking and disobedience. But side by side with these negative facets, there now appears man's positive endeavor to submit totally and joyfully to the will of God. Only when man thus

[8] Cf. E. Neuhäusler, *Anspruch und Antwort Gottes* (Düsseldorf, 1962), 125–140. The author stresses that Jesus' call for repentance thus assumes a different character from that of John the Baptist, who stays within the framework of Old Testament prophecy.

places his own existence into God's hands, at God's disposition, is he freed from the constriction and bondage of his ego. God himself holds out his hand to man: He wants to establish his kingdom of salvation, and calls man to approach and commune with him.

To this demand for conversion there is joined the summons to have faith in the salvation message. It is like an interpretation: the conversion that is here demanded is accomplished by faith, and faith in turn is a conversion. Here lies the decisive difference between Jesus' call for conversion, and that of John the Baptist: Jesus demands conversion because the kingdom of God is already a palpable reality. For Jesus, the convert's attitude consists no longer in preparing for God's kingdom, but in answering to God's act of salvation. Mark 10:15 calls on man to "receive the kingdom of God like a child"; here the assumption is that the kingdom of God is in fact a present reality.[9] For to have faith means just this: to accept Jesus' message and demand with childlike simplicity. In this sense, faith itself is conversion, is the positive element in conversion, obedience to the voice of God that has become audible through Jesus. Such conversion in faith requires that man give himself over to God, that he surrender in trust and obedience to Him who is forever above us, and who wills our best.

[9] Cf. R. Schnackenburg, *God's Rule and Kingdom* (New York, 1963).

Like John the Baptist before him, so Jesus, too, calls for a conversion which, although one single act, is valid for all times. A relapse would be worse than the state before conversion (cf. Lk 11:26). But to Christ, the unique character of man's turning toward God is due not so much to the irrevocability of the imminent judgment, as it was for John—but rather to the definitive arrival of God's kingdom. And the kingdom of God calls for another morality, for a righteousness which exceeds that of the scribes and Pharisees (Mt 5:20). It calls for the will to become perfect, for sincere service down into the most hidden recesses of the human heart, for brotherly love to the very foundations of man's character, and even for love of one's enemy, after God's example (cf. Mt 5–7). This makes it clear why the children of God can be asked not only to be free of all that is sinful, but even to surrender goods of this world that in themselves are valuable if such surrender seems necessary "for the sake of the kingdom of heaven" (Mt 19:12; Lk 9:62; 14:26). Conversion, once it has been achieved in principle, must again and again be actualized, applied, and proved in the concrete situations of this world.

Jesus knows that such renunciation of the good things of this life, for the sake of complete concentration on God, is hard and at times too hard—and yet he does not yield one inch. He himself has experienced the demonic power of riches among men, which keeps so many from entering God's kingdom. When he expresses his view, in the hard saying about the camel and the eye of a needle, his disciples are exceedingly disturbed; but Jesus looked at them and said, "With men it is impossible (that man be saved), but not with God" (Mk 10:25–27).[10] If we consider that conversion is at the root of that renunciation of wealth which Christ demands, it here becomes clear that conversion is in the last analysis *God's grace,* a power that man must receive from God.

Starting with Jesus' call "Repent and Believe" (Mk 1:15), we may consider conversion as the decisive attitude that is required to enter into God's kingdom; conversion thus might be called the "central concept" of the attitude which Jesus demands.[11] But it is better to give the *central* place in Jesus' demand to love of God and neighbor, and to leave conversion to its *fundamental* function. Its fundamental importance arises from the fact that the world has entered into the *kairos* of God's kingdom. Since God's kingdom is near, a decision must be made: the decision to shake ourselves loose from our bondage to self and to

[10] This context (question of wealth) could also reflect concern within the community over Jesus' sharp words against wealth. Yet the thought that humanly impossible things become possible with God's help is expressed also in others of Jesus' sayings which clearly bear the mark of his spirit: the sayings of the faith that moves mountains; and of the prayers certain to be answered. Mk 11:23, 24).

[11] Cf. Pohlmann's work cited in Note 2 above.

the world, and to submit in faith and obedience and love to the will of God that Christ proclaims.

THE PENITENTIAL SERMON IN THE EARLY CHURCH: THE ACTS OF THE APOSTLES

The early Church, heir to Jesus' bequest and charged to carry on his work—how did it take up the call for conversion and integrate it in its message? We know that in the early Church there occurred a shift in the principal stress of the message of salvation as compared with Jesus' time; Jesus' preaching of the kingdom of God receded, while the message of Jesus the Messiah and son of God moved into the foreground.[12] The Church was under the necessity to widen the time gap between the beginning of God's rule in Jesus and its completion in the kingdom of God: because this time between is the time span of the Church's own activity. That endeavor finds its strongest expression in the theology of Luke, to whom we also owe the Acts of the Apostles. How is conversion conceived here, and how is Jesus' demand taken up and carried on?

In the Acts, too, conversion means a total change of man's disposition, a turning toward God who calls men to salvation, and who gives salvation (cf. Acts 3:19; 26:20). What is meant, first, in line with the prophets of the Old Testament, is *moral* conversion, a giving up of every

[12] Cf. Schnackenburg, *God's Rule and Kingdom.*

sinful and wrongful attitude; we see it especially in Peter's words to Simon Magus: "Repent therefore of this wickedness of yours!" (8:22), and in the admonition to his Jewish audience: "Repent therefore, and turn again, that your sins may be blotted out!" (3:19). But what is envisaged more often is *religious* conversion (cf. 9:35; 11:21), a turning of man's faith. It is not a mere change of confession but, on the contrary, demands a fundamentally new understanding of salvation, a fundamentally new relation to God offering salvation through Christ. Conversion is now closely linked with *faith* in Jesus whom men have crucified, but whom God has resurrected, raised to sit at God's right hand, and made "both Lord and Christ" (Acts 2:34–36).[13] In this sense Paul, speaking to the elders in Miletus, states the content of his teaching both to Jews and pagans: conversion to God and faith in our Lord Jesus Christ (20:21); similarly in his defense before King Agrippa (26:18–20). Conversion in this all-inclusive sense is demanded as the essential condition

---

[13] Cf. Acts 2:34–36; 5:31 f.; 10:39–43; 13:26–41. On the penitential sermon in the Acts of the Apostles, see J. Dupont, "Repentir et conversion d'après les Actes des Apôtres," *Sciences Ecclésiastiques,* 12 (1960), 137–173; R. Koch, "Die religiös-sittliche Umkehr (μετάνοια) nach den drei ältesten Evangelien und der Apostelgeschichte," *Anima* 14 (1959), 296–307; generally in the early Church: W. Lange, "L'appel à la pénitence dans le christianisme primitif," *Collectanea Mechliniensia* 44 (1959), 380–390.

to receive baptism. And Peter in his Pentecostal sermon answers the men who ask, What shall we do?, with these words: "Repent, and be baptized every one of you in the name of Jesus Christ for the forgiveness of your sins!" (2:38). At Christian baptism, conversion has still another meaning besides the meaning at John's baptism which Acts 13:24 and 19:4 recall. The forgiveness of sin is an effect of baptism in the Christian Spirit; conversion, in turn, includes faith—the acceptance of Jesus Christ as the sole mediator of salvation. Through baptism, man becomes a member of his eschatological community of salvation.

The call for conversion addressed to the *Jews* of that time gains special meaning further through its position in the history of salvation. In the view of Luke, the Jews are burdened by this guilt, that they have hardened their hearts against the voice of Jesus the Messiah, God's last emissary, and that they—or at least their official representatives and leaders—have brought him to the cross and killed him. They must understand that this was the wrong decision, and must repent, even though they and their rulers acted in ignorance (3:17 ff.). God has raised this same Jesus from the dead, and now offers to the Jews the last opportunity to accept his salvation which they have declined so far. And Luke also looks toward the eschatological future. The Jews are called to conversion, so "that times of refreshing may come from the presence of the Lord, and that he may send the Christ appointed for you, Jesus, whom heaven

must receive until the time for establishing all
that God spoke" (3:19 ff.).[14] The conversion call
thus achieves unprecedented urgency; it is directed to the present, personal, special situation
of the Jews, and appeals to motives that are
close to them. The Gentiles, by contrast, are
reminded by Paul (in his sermon on the Areopagus) of the judgment over all the world to which
Jesus has been appointed (17:30). Nobody is
exempt from the call to conversion, whatever his
spiritual and religious antecedents. God's summons touches every man, although it must be
carried to each man in keeping with his situation
and condition.

We also encounter the thought in the Acts that
conversion is a gift of God, or of God's spirit, to
Jews (5:31) as much as Gentiles (11:18). In
his speech before the council—when many Jews
in Jerusalem had already joined the community

[14] In this passage it is controversial whether Luke has
adopted an ancient christological view; cf. O. Bau-
ernfeind, "Tradition und Komposition in dem Apo-
katastasis-Spruch Apg 3:20 f." in *Abraham unser
Vater* (*Festschrift für O. Michel*) (Leiden-Cologne,
1963), 13–23; F. Hahn, *Christologische Hoheitstitel*
(Göttingen, 1963), 184–186. But there is no need to
assume a view different from that elsewhere in the
Acts; Jesus has been destined and given to the Jews
as their messiah, and as such is ready in heaven (cf.
2:36) to bring about the time of salvation. See G.
Voss, *Die Christologie der lukanischen Schriften in
Grundzügen* (Paris and Bruges, 1965), 28–31, 151 f.

of Christ—Peter consciously presents this "repent-ance" of Israel as the work of God, intended to show to the rulers of the people their guilty hard-ness of heart, and their opposition to God's will. They, the rulers, are obstinate—in contrast with the majority of the people. Later, Peter invokes the witness of the Holy Spirit "whom God has given to those who obey him" (5:32). Similarly, the converted Jews recognize God's work in the vision coming to the Gentile Cornelius and his household, by which God gives to the Gentiles, too, "conversion to life." The early Church is con-scious even then of having entered the time of Messianic fulfillment; and with all its missionary activity in the world, it yet considers itself the work of God's grace, and of the Spirit.

THE RECEDENCE OF THE IDEA OF CONVERSION WITH PAUL AND JOHN

The early church, then, ties conversion ever more firmly to the acceptance of the faith in Christ and membership in the community of Christ. This does not mean, of course, that conversion now becomes an outward change of faith. On the con-trary, the early church stresses the importance of man's inner turning toward God, and the role of God's grace. To become a Christian is more that a mere reappraisal of one's stance toward the world, and more than a mere ethical reawakening: it is a supernatural rebirth which must express itself in a corresponding conduct of life. These thoughts came to maturity with Paul and John, though each formulated them in his own way. For both of them, the conversion call recedes into the background—outwardly, as a concept; but in effect it remains present, implicit in the call to have faith, and effective in the moral imperative. Conversion is understood in a more profound sense than that of a break with one's present life, and a new start toward a life of sanctity and love. Conversion draws its deepest strength from the spirit of God which comes to the faithful convert as a gift of God.

Paul's most profound statements about *metanoia,* accordingly, are not those in which he talks about the repentance of "impurity, immorality, and licentiousness" (2 Cor 12:21), or warns of God's impending judgment and points out that it is God's kindness which leads men to repentance (Rom 2:4). Paul's central thought is found in those passages where he contrasts the former conduct of his audience with their present ways in purity and sanctity—ways that have become possible for them through the grace of God, through redemption by Jesus Christ, and by the power of the Holy Spirit.[15] Paul is inspired with the reality of the new creation: "The old has passed away; behold the new has come" (2 Cor 5:12). However, this new life in Christ places the Christians under an obligation to act in keeping with the new nature

---

[15] Cf. 1 Cor 6:9–11; Eph 2:3–7; Col 1:21–23; 2:13; 2 Thess 2:13.

that is theirs through baptism, and to conduct themselves according to the spirit that gives them life. (Gal 5:25; Rom 8:12) Since in the reality of grace they have with Christ become dead to the powers of sin, sin is no longer to reign in their mortal bodies (Rom 6:12 ff.). It is impossible to define more sharply the completely new orientation of life for which he calls; but Paul does not call his central demand "conversion"; he uses other expressions: Men shall not live according to the flesh, they shall walk in the spirit, put on the new man. . . . It would seem that he is avoiding a concept which played a large part in the old covenant. Most of all, Paul's ethics is based on the new life in Christ, which is an accomplished fact. The decision to believe in Christ, once it is made, and the new life in Christ which God has established, ought to be so powerful that a relapse into the ways of the past is simply impossible (Col 3:7; Eph 2:2 f; 5:8). Only on one occasion does Paul speak of a "repentance" that leads the Corinthian community "to salvation," through the grief that his reproachful letter was bound to cause them (2 Cor 7:9 f.). But that is in a special context. That radical reappraisal of human existence which Paul refrains from calling "conversion" even though that is what it is, consists for him in faith in the Crucified; the Christian must be crucified with Christ in order that he may also rise with Christ.[16] A Christian

[16] On this Pauline thought of being crucified with Christ, cf. R. Schnackenburg, *Baptism in the Thought*

who has not consciously taken this step, who has not made the decision to live with Christ, has not yet achieved conversion in Paul's sense.

In the gospel according to *John,* the word does not occur at all. It has become absorbed in the rich and all-embracing idea of faith. By believing in Christ the Son, man seizes salvation, and receives divine life (for example, 3:16 and 36,). Such faith is personal attitude and existential enactment. In faith, man turns his back on all things that are counter to God, on darkness and death, and fixes his eyes on the divine salvation that has appeared in Christ—fixes his eyes on Christ himself, the bearer of light and life. Faith includes obedience (3:36), and keeping Christ's words and commandments (8:51; 12:47; 14:21, 23). The sharp contrast which John establishes between God's world filled with light and life, and the dark universe of death, expresses the radical break that occurs in the life of the be-

of St. Paul (Oxford, 1964); A. Wikenhauser, *Pauline Mysticism* (Freiburg, 1960); Ph. Seidensticker, *Lebendiges Opfer* (Münster, 1954), 233–263; P. Bonnard, "Mourir et vivre avec Jésus-Christ selon s. Paul," *Revue d'Histoire et de Philosophie Religieuse* 36 (1956), 101–112; A. Feuillet, "Mort du Christ et mort du chrétien d'après les épîtres paulin" *RB* 66 (1959), 481–513, esp. 491–496; E. Schweizer, "Die 'Mystik' des Sterbens und Auferstehens mit Christus bei Paulus," *Evangelische Theologie* 26 (1966), 239–257; R. Tannehill, *Dying and Rising with Christ* (Berlin, 1966). See also Chapter 4, below, on "The Imitation of Christ."

liever: he has passed from death to life (5:24). In the face of Christ, there is no third choice other than belief or unbelief.[17] Belief means salvation; while unbelief, which cloaks evil's flight from the light of the good, is in fact the judgment (3:18–21). In this way, faith according to John includes that conversion of which the synoptic Jesus speaks. That the fourth evangelist no longer employs that term may be because he, even more than Paul, has detached himself from Judaism and Jewish ways of thinking. The fundamental reason, however, is his Christological concentration: Christ, the way by which man comes to God the Father, is comprehended only by faith—but faith comprehends him fully and completely (14:6–11). He who believes in Christ has made his decision, for God and against God's opponents, for love and against hatred, and that is the true core of conversion.[18]

The unique and irrevocable nature of the decision which constitutes conversion and faith in Christ is stressed with special emphasis in the Letter to the Hebrews. That complete reversal must express itself in the thinking and conduct of the Christian. The writer of the Letter does not want to lay again "a foundation of repent-

[17] Cf. Jn 1:11 f.; 3:18, 36 f.; 6:36 f.; 12:46 f.
[18] Cf. R. Schnackenburg, *The Moral Teaching of the New Testament* (New York, 1965); N. Lazure, *Les valeurs morales de la théologie johannique* (Paris, 1965), 182–200.

ance from dead works and of faith toward God, with instruction about ablutions, the laying on of hands, the resurrection of the dead, and eternal judgment" (6:1-2). Next, in a famous passage, he states that it is impossible to restore to repentance those who have committed apostasy (6:4-6). We must note the high view the writer takes of the condition of being a Christian. To be a Christian is to him something altogether new, unsurpassable, an anticipation of the blessings of the world to come. He uses four expressions to describe this experience: Christians have once been enlightened, they have tasted the heavenly gift, and have become partakers of the Holy Spirit, and have tasted the goodness of the word of God, and the powers of the age to come (6:3 f.). The thought of man's relapse from this salvation into the abyss of unbelief and sin is so intolerable to the author of the Letter that he considers it beyond the power of any prophet or teacher to recall an apostate to repentance. No claim is made that it is beyond the power of God's grace, although the author does not seem to hold out much hope for such divine intervention. In any case, in 12:17 he says that Esau, after he sold his birthright, found "no chance to repent," even though he sought it with tears. A total apostasy from the Christian faith, the writer believes, is as though such men crucified the Son of God on their own account and held him up to contempt (6:6). While these shattering terms must not be applied to every "mortal sin" in the catalogue—1 John 5:16

59

means by "sin unto death" a particularly grave guilt which we can no longer specifically define[19] —yet this view will make clear to us the full seriousness of the decision to embrace Christian faith and life, the full responsibility of being a Christian.

THE FINAL CONVERSION SERMON IN THE NEW TESTAMENT: THE APOCALYPSE OF JOHN

In the first flush of his conversion to Christianity, and in his passionate devotion to the Lord, Paul was convinced that all new Christians must feel about the new beginning in their life just as he did, and surrender themselves totally as the Lord's willing captives; but he, and all the exalted heralds of the Christian message of salvation that came after him, had to realize that the converts to Christ did not entirely give up their old ways. What is discouraging is not only the moral weakness which causes man to relapse into sin again

[19] See the Commentaries for the various proposed explanations. N. Lazure, *loc. cit.*, 310–314, suggests that it means the sin that leads to killing, that is, hatred. This is a profound idea, which appears to be in harmony with John's concepts of love and hate (cf. 1 Jn 3:14 f.); but it does not explain why this "sin unto death" is excepted from the prayer for one's brothers (5:16). It would be against the commandment to love our enemies, as Jesus gave it (Lk 6:27 f.). "Sin unto death" probably means rather that inner "sickness unto death" (cf. Jn 11:4) which drives its victim to his own (eternal) death.

and again; for these sins of weakness we have "an advocate with the Father, Jesus Christ the righteous" (1 Jn 2:1). Much more alarming is the fact that the enthusiasm of faith, the love of Christ, is fading. The very core of conversion, the uncompromising decision for God, is here endangered. A moral failure before the world's temptations, in the exhausting struggle against human frailty, can be overcome with the help of God's spirit, if only man holds fast to his fundamental rejection of all evil and to his loving reverence for God in the community of Christ. But if the inner drive of a living Christian faith dies down, Christian vital force dries up at the source. In his own day, the visionary of the New Testament had already observed in his communities that same weakening of the love they held at first, that same cooling of the heart which is so frightening to us today, and with his apocalyptic vision recognized it as one of the greatest dangers. In the expectation of the rapidly approaching end of the world, he therefore summons his communities once more to convert and repent, even though they had been practicing Christians for some time; and his call is one of ruthless frankness and burning urgency. This is the final form of conversion sermon in the New Testament, closely related to the manner of the ancient prophets and yet completely Christian in expression. It draws its most powerful themes from the conviction that the coming of the Lord is imminent.

"But I have this against you, that you have

abandoned the love you had at first. Remember then from what you have fallen, repent and do the works you did at first. If not, I will come to you and remove your lampstand from its place, unless you repent" (Rev 2:4–5). What is meant is not that Christians must repent constantly afresh; but the fundamental, inalterably valid conversion needs to be renewed and revitalized in vigorous impulses, before the coming of the Lord. The prospect of the parousia, clearly, fires the call for conversion. This renewed turning toward Christ is a necessity, lest the community of Ephesus be punished by the Lord himself when he comes. Through the mouth of his visionary, the Lord calls on the community of Pergamon to give up superstition. They must not tolerate any member who holds the teachings of the Nicolaitans. "Repent then. If not, I will come to you soon and war against them [the schismatic members of the community] with the sword of my mouth" (2:16). Even though many good things can be found—for example in Thyatira, love and faith and service and patient endurance—it is not enough. All things un-Christian, all things pagan must be uprooted. "I gave her [the sinful harlot and her suitors in the community] time to repent, but she refuses to repent of her immorality.[20] Behold, I will throw

[20] The passage probably refers also to the false doctrine of the Nicolaitans who, in the message to Pergamum (2:14) as well as here (2:20), are accused of immorality and of eating food sacrificed to idols.

her on a sickbed, and those who commit adultery with her I will throw into great tribulations, unless they repent of her doings" (2:21 f.). Their watchfulness must not be half-way, for such is the sleep of death. And that is how the visionary sees the condition of the community of Sardis. "Remember then what you received and heard; keep that, and repent. If you will not awake, I will come like a thief . . ." (3:3). The tribulations of the last days are salutary chastisements of God, intended to fill the lukewarm with a renewed ardor of faith and love. The community of Laodicea, whose works are neither cold nor hot, are to be shaken from their slumber by apocalyptic terror: "So be zealous and repent" (3:19). In the thunderstorm of the final events, the community is to shake off all half-heartedness, all mediocrity. And as the battle between God and Satan rises to its climax, and the community of Christ is set upon by the great red dragon (Ch. 12) and his terrestrial helpmates, no man can stand aside and lead a satisfied and comfortable life.

Even God's eschatological judgment, which the

We probably have to do with some gnostic-libertinistic aberration spread in Thyatira by a "prophetess" (with the symbolic name Jezebel). Thus the language is not merely symbolic: such aberrations did in fact occur among the Christian communities; and the Lord threatened that they would be punished with sickness for the "prophetess" who seduced the people to immorality, and with great tribulations for her followers. Cf. the Commentaries.

visionary shows in his visions of the seven trumpets and the seven bowls, could still at the last moment lead to repentance those men who will be witnesses to those terrors. But John notes (9:20 f.; 16:9, 11) that those men who survive after the apocalyptic host has swept the earth, or after the bowls of wrath have been emptied—these men do not repent but only curse God all the more. It seems, then, that even the most fearful terror will not produce miracles of repentance. A man who does not recognize the "signs of the times" and is not led by them to think and to repent, such a man is in danger of hardening into an obduracy which no outside events will overcome ever again.

The visionary preacher of Patmos sees his era approaching the dramatic events of the world's end, and wants to prepare his communities for what is to come.[21] This is the last chance for his communities in Asia Minor to achieve that inner attitude and frame of mind which will be needed

[21] On the eschatological stance of the prophet, his expectation of the world's end, and his view of time and history, cf. L. Goppelt, "Heilsoffenbarung und Geschichte nach der Offenbarung des Johannes," *Theologische Literaturzeitung* 77 (1952), 513–522; P. Häring, *Die Botschaft der Offenbarung des hl. Johannes* (Munich, 1953); H. Schlier, "Zum Verständnis der Geschichte nach der Offenbarung Johannis," *Die Zeit der Kirche* (Freiburg, 1956), 265–287; M. Rissi, *Time and History* (Richmond, 1966); A. Feuillet, *L'Apocalypse. État de la question* (Paris-Bruges, 1963), 31–52, 62–65 (with literature).

to meet the trials and sufferings of the final days, the assault of hell with all its powers. The battle is not yet lost for the weak, the lukewarm, and half-hearted, provided they repent. Each exhortation ends with a pledge of victory: to those who do not falter in the battle against evil, and hold out on God's side through all the persecutions of the present day, the heavenly Lord promises his reward and his laurel crown.

This sermon of repentance in the Apocalypse also still brings to mind Jesus' proclamation: "The time is fulfilled, and the kingdom of God is at hand; repent, and believe in the gospel" (Mk 1:15). The last evangelist of the New Testament, however, has turned Jesus' message into a concrete summons to his contemporaries. He understood that the eschatological moment retains its urgency, and that the fiery signs of the times might turn it into the world's end. His apocalyptic vision shows him that "the time is near" (Rev 1:3; 22:10), although he does not indicate the exact moment. The daily events, the outburst of a pogrom which has already claimed many Christian lives, the idolization of the state and the worship of the Emperor, all these seem the beginning of the mighty tribulations just before the end. Still, the precise moment is not what matters most, but the eschatological disposition of the Christians, "the endurance and faith of the saints" (13:10). And that was indeed the true concern of Jesus in everything he said about the kingdom of God being "at hand": to keep his disciples alert and ready, strong in courage and faith.[22] All these "eschatological virtues" have their root in repentance rightly understood; for the man who turns wholly to God, and guides himself by God alone, does not fear whatever is to come, but faces the future with courage and calm, hope and anticipation. The future is God's; whenever and in whatever way the "end" may come, it brings divine perfection, God's kingdom in its glory.

We have now reached a point where there is meaning for us even in so apocalyptic, time-bound, and obscure a piece of writing as the last book of the New Testament. There is more at stake here than merely a call to repentance addressed to a sorely tried community, in expectation of the impending end of the world, whom the prophet is warning of the terrors of the end to come as he sees them in his compact vision. What is at stake here is the Christian existential situation generally in this world, which is depicted here with the stylistic resources of the Apocalypse. In the world of history, and in the world's history, the Christian cannot come face to face with the last things, the things that hold his salvation. He is placed within the world, he takes an active part in it—but he knows what he owes to him who made the world and who is guiding history toward its end, toward salvation in Christ. And this subordination of his existence, of his whole life to God is precisely what the New Testament calls "conversion."

[22] See the final essay in the sequel to the present volume, "The Christian and the Future of the World."

III

The Meaning of Faith in the Bible

It cannot be denied that modern man finds it difficult to feel a living and strong religious faith. We cannot trace here the causes and expressions of this difficulty. But we are prompted to turn to the Bible and ask ourselves if this book of revelation and of faith par excellence might not give faith a new, fresh impetus.[1]

[1] The only monograph on faith throughout the New Testament is by a Protestant author, A. Schlatter, *Der Glaube im Neuen Testament* (Stuttgart, 1927; reissued Darmstadt, 1963). A good survey will be found in the article by A. Weiser and R. Bultmann in *ThWNT* VI (Stuttgart, 1959), 174–230. From Catholic authors we have only the older discussion by P. Antoine in *Dictionnaire de la Bible,* Suppl. III (Paris, 1938), 276–310. Other works deal with individual authors, in particular with Paul and John; see the pertinent sections in the textbooks of New Testament theology. With reference to Paul, see: E. Wissman, *Das Verhältnis von Pistis und Christusfrömmigkeit bei Paulus* (Göttingen, 1926); W. Mundle, *Der Glaubensbegriff des Paulus* (Leipzig, 1932); O. Kuss,

We are here not so much interested in the content of faith (*fides quae creditur*) as in the act of faith and inner disposition of faith (*fides qua creditur*), although the two can hardly be separated, and affect each other. Today's biblical scholarship lends promise to our enterprise in various ways. Scholarship today pays greater attention to the religious dispositions and the theological content of Scripture than it did formerly; it traces more carefully the specific modes of thinking in Scripture which show such striking similarity to today's existential trends in thought and action; indeed, it has come to take a different view of the biblical documents themselves. These documents are no longer regarded as books of revelation which, so

Der Römerbrief, 1st section (Regensburg, 1957), 131–154; H. Ljungman, *Pistis. A Study of Its Presuppositions and Its Meaning in Pauline Use* (Lund, 1964); A. Terstiege, *Hoffen und Glauben* (Rome, 1964); J. Gnilka, *Paulus und unser christlicher Glaube: Lebendiges Zeugnis* (Paderborn, 1964), 46–56. With reference to John, see: J. Huby, "La connaissance de foi dans s. Jean," *Recherches de Science Religieuse* 21 (1931), 385–421; D. Mollat, "La foi dans le quatrième évangile," in *Lumière et Vie* 22 (1955), 515–531; M. Bonningues, *La foi dans l'Évangile de s. Jean* (Paris, 1955); W. Grundmann, "Verständnis und Bewegung des Glaubens im Johannesevangelium," in *Einsicht und Glaube (Festschrift für G. Söhngen)* (Freiburg i.Br., 1962), 96–111; R. Schnackenburg, *Das Johannesevangelium* I (Freiburg i.Br., 1965), 508–524.

to speak, descended out of the clouds; they are rather historical statements of faith written by men who shared the intellectual framework of their times; in part they reflect the faith of the community from which they stem, and in part they also betray the personal vision, and the vigor of their authors' faith. Yet Catholic exegesis does by no means exclude that God and his Holy Spirit inspire this process in which the insights and confessions of faith are collected, handed on, written down and organized. Catholic exegesis holds that the Bible contains the sole and only true revelation of God in the history of mankind. But it also sees with growing clarity that this revelation is dependent upon an economy of salvation, upon the ongoing history of revelation leading up to Jesus Christ, upon the historically conditioned acceptance of the revelation by men, and its preservation and presentation by men once more: In short, that revelation is dependent upon the historical partnership of man. Seen in this light, adapted to the Bible's nature as a work that is both human and divine, the individual books begin to speak to us directly as witnesses of faith, and to allow us insights into the beliefs of the community and the author at the same time as they convey to us their content of revelation. Thus we shall give close attention to what the Bible says about the meaning of "faith," and also to the frame of mind of the people whom we meet in these writings. In the present context, we can deal with a selection only; we further mean to emphasize certain

traits which may have been slighted in our cate-
chism for reasons we shall not go into.

THE KINDS OF FAITH IN THE BIBLE

We note first of all that in the Bible the verb
predominates rather than the noun, that the Bible
speaks of "to believe" rather than of "faith"; this
alone is an indication of the importance the
Bible attaches to faithful conduct (*fides qua creditur*).[2] On closer study, we see that this "faith"
absorbs the whole man, with all his powers. To
have faith means in the Bible to submit one's
whole person to God in humility and trust, in surrender and obedience, in thought and in deed.
The thing which we tend to stress most—the firm
conviction of the truth of God's revelation—appears in the Bible rather as a partial aspect, important to be sure, but not entitled to be emphasized
exclusively or to be made the sole valid yardstick.
Otherwise, there is the danger that we shall separate the revelation from the God who reveals himself, and who wants to appeal to man and move
him to respond. We understand more fully today
that the biblical revelation is not mere information

[2] The somewhat different approach, the greater emphasis on the "existential" attitude of faith is reflected in the little book *Glauben Heute*, published
by J. M. Reuss in Mainz, 1962; it is composed of
papers given at a conference on pastoral theology.
This essay, in a somewhat different form, was first
published in that book, pp. 13–35.

about hidden matters, but rather God's self-com-
munication made for our salvation.[3] Man's proper
response, which God expects, is faith. Thus revelation achieves its real purpose only where it leads
to an encounter of man with God; according to the
Bible, the true core of faith conduct is in the
answer which man makes to God from his heart
of hearts. In the face of God, man is summoned
directly, and by believing makes his decision to
answer God's claim on him. That decision includes the firm conviction of the truth of revelation, and its affirmation by the will; but it also
includes trust in God, surrender to him, and above
all a personal loyalty to him. The faith of the Bible
is a total loyalty of man to God, which must be
adopted consciously, and renewed again and again
until it becomes a definitive attitude. The Bible
does not try to define faith, and we do not mean
to do so either. Even the famous passage in
Hebrew 11:1 is not a definition; according to

[3] On recent theological discussions concerning "revelation," see H. Fries in *Mysterium Salutis* I, ed. J.
Feiner and M. Löhrer (Einsiedeln, 1965), 159–234
(with bibliography pp. 235–238). Cf. also the dog-
matic constitution of Vatican II on divine revelation,
which states: "By his divine revelation, God wished
to make known himself and the eternal decrees of his
will concerning the salvation of man, 'to let man
share in the divine riches which simply surpass the
capacities of the human spirit'" (No. 6); see also
O. Semmelroth and M. Zerwick, *Vaticanum II über
das Wort Gottes* (Stuttgart, 1966), 69.

recent studies, the difficult phrases should be translated about like this: "Faith endows the things which we hope for with the full certainty of future realization; faith endows the things which we do not see with the full certainty of proof."[4] The passage, then, merely stresses certain partial aspects, at the beginning of a long list of shining examples of faith (Ch. 11), in order to underline the need for faith and the power of faith. However, let us first turn to the Old Testament.

"Faith" in the Old Testament

It might be thought surprising that we do not read very often of "faith" in the Old Testament; but when we do, it is a *living* relation to God, and thus it is mentioned mainly on occasions when this relation is put to the test. The first example we encounter is *Abraham*. God promises to the aged patriarch that he will give him a son, and that his descendants will be as numerous as the stars in the sky. "And he believed the Lord; and he reckoned it to him as righteousness" (Gen 15:6). It is well known that Paul seized on this example in Romans 4, to explain the way to salvation through faith, as against the way through good works. But more important

---

[4] H. Dörrie, "Zu Hebr. 11, 1," *Zeitschrift für die neutestamentliche Wissenschaft* 46 (1955), 196–202, citation 202. Cf. E. Grässer, *Der Glaube im Hebräerbrief* (Marburg, 1965), 46–53.

for our purposes is that Paul uses the example, at the end of Chapter 4 (vv. 17–25), to show what true faith is like. It is a faith in a God "who gives life to the dead and calls into existence the things that do not exist." Here is revealed one of the basic traits of biblical faith: it clings to a God who is infinitely greater and more powerful than man, and who can help and save even where man's wisdom and power fails. There is something paradoxical about such a faith, as Paul points up with his striking phrase, "In hope he believed against hope"; in God-given hope he believed, against all human hope. Nor must we fail to notice that the apostle applies the example of Abraham directly to Christian faith: We believe in him who has raised Jesus, our Lord, from the dead (4:23)!

It could be that we are no longer sufficiently aware of this irrational and paradoxical aspect of our faith in Christ, because the foundations laid by fundamental theology, useful and necessary as they are, give us too much rational security, or at least the illusion of security. And yet: is not our entire faith in Christ dependent on this God who raises the dead? And are there not in such a faith forces which prove especially effective in trials and tribulations? The moments when man's faith is challenged are the moments when he needs something of the kind of biblical faith. He will conquer a crisis more readily once he has experienced the joy that fills a faithful heart when it encounters God in all his wonderful power and kindness. Thus the song of praise of Hannah, mother of Samuel: "The Lord kills and brings to life; he brings down to the Sheol and raises up. . . . He raises up the poor from the dust; he lifts the needy from the ash heap" (1 Samuel 2:6 ff.)— thoughts which Mary, called blessed because of her faith, includes in her *Magnificat* (Lk 1:45–55). Mary's faith, too, was such a submission to God's inscrutable mystery; but the theme which the angel mentions to her ("with God nothing will be impossible," Lk 1:37), was familiar to a woman of her nation. The aged Tobias, too, expresses himself similarly in his song of praise: "Lord, you wield the scourge and you give the cure; you lead into the realm of death, and out again" (Tob 13:2). And finally there is Paul once more, after his escape from mortal danger: "Why, we felt that we had received the sentence of death; but that was to make us rely not on ourselves but on God who raises the dead" (2 Cor 1:9).

The same manner of faith appears, both as a fact and as an imperative, in the *history of God's people*. After its salvation from the sea of reeds, it says: "The people feared the Lord; and they believed in the Lord and in his servant Moses" (Ex 14:31). Psalm 106 first castigates the people's rebellion, their lack of faith in the God who led them out of Egypt, but then it says: "Then they believed his words; they sang his praise" (v. 12). These are landmarks in Israel's encounter with its God, firmly placed in history. The theophany on Mount Sinai is another (see Ex 19:9). And conversely, the people's murmuring in the desert is reproved as a lack of faith.[5] Its faith in God is experienced by the people of Israel in history as a vital allegiance to the lord. The times of humiliation and national disaster are understood as punishment for lack of faith and loyalty to Yahweh, and thus give rise to a call for renewed trust and reliance upon the God of salvation.

Even the terminology betrays it. The Hebrew term for "believing" (*he' emīn*) comes from the root word *'aman,* to be firm, and means "to know yourself secure, to hold to someone, to rely on someone." It has rightly been said that such faith is a "saying *Amen* to God."[6] It means to affirm and accept his greatness, kindness, and wisdom, to submit to his will, to trust and obey him in confidence and hope. This interpretation is confirmed by a large number of related verbs, such as "to take refuge." "It is better to take refuge in the Lord than to put confidence in princes" (Ps 118:8; cf. Ps 25:20; 57:2; 61:4; 91:4). Such faith leads man to be near God, to communion with him (Ps 73:28), and gives man certainty of God's help (Ps 33:18 f. and 20 ff; 40:2 ff.) and hope of God's salvation (Ps 119:41 f.).

The *prophetic sermon,* too, insists that the faithful must take their stand with God, and rely on him absolutely.[7] At those times when the peo-

[5] Num 14:11; 20:12; Deut 1:32.

[6] A. Weiser in *ThWNT* VI, 187, 3 f.

[7] Cf. also W. Eichrodt, *Theology of the Old Testament* II–III (Philadelphia, 1961–1967); G. von Rad, *Old Testament Theology,* Vol. II (New York, 1962–1965).

ple forgot its God, the prophets, men of God, assumed the role of critic to scourge the lack of piety. Jeremiah accuses his people of placing a mistaken trust in idols and things of this world (Jer 5:17; 7:4, 8, 14; 13:25; 17:5). When Amos (6:1) cries out: "Woe to those who are at ease in Zion, and to those who feel secure on the mountain of Samaria!"—he cries out against lack of faith. Hosea (10:13 f.) castigates false self-confidence: "Because you have trusted in your chariots and in the multitude of your warriors, therefore the tumult of war shall arise among your people, and all your fortresses shall be destroyed." Habakkuk says that "the righteous shall live by his faith" (Hab 2:4). And Isaiah (7:9) in the hour of need when Jerusalem was besieged, said the tremendous words: "If you will not believe, surely you shall not be established." This precisely is faith: to take one's stand with God, to be established in him, especially in the hour of tribulation and decision. This is what makes Isaiah the "prophet of faith"—that he teaches faith in the hidden God of salvation which will withstand distress and darkness. "I will wait for the Lord, who is hiding his face from the house of Jacob, and I will hope in Him" (8:17). These words express the inner attitude of the faithful in the hour of darkness.

Out of this attitude grows the faith of eschatological hope. "It will be said on that day, 'Lo, this is our God; we have waited for him, that he might save us. This is the Lord; we have waited for him; let us be glad and rejoice in his salvation' " (Is 25:9).[8] This rejoicing comes fully to the fore especially in Deutero-Isaiah, the great prophet of salvation: "They who wait for the Lord shall renew their strength, they shall mount up with wings likes eagles" (40:31). But it presupposes that man take a large view of God. Only where God is conceived in his supernatural greatness, only where he is known as the good and loyal God who seeks man's salvation, only there can his promise be heard: "He who takes refuge in me shall possess the land, and shall inherit my holy mountain" (57:13).

"Faith" in the New Testament

The New Testament, as we have seen, continues this Old Testament concept of faith. In Jesus' life, we encounter faith first in connection with the cures of the sick. Men are expected to believe that God's helping power is present in Jesus. To the woman with the issue of blood (Mk 5:34) and the blind Bartimaeus, Jesus gives the assurance: "Your faith has made you well." And when

---

[8] The passage belongs to the so-called "Isaiah Apocalypse," one of the oldest documents on the matter. Cf. O. Plöger, *Theokratie und Eschatologie* (Neukirchen, 1959), 69–97. On our passage, he writes: "It is an expression of trust, in the form of a short song of thanksgiving; and in view of the special importance that Zion has in the eschatological event, it speaks even now of Yahweh's sheltering and caressing hand" (p. 79).

the ruler of the synagogue, Jairus, receives the
news of his daughter's death, Jesus says to him:
"Do not fear, only believe" (Mk 5:36). Such
faith is the devoted trust in the God of salvation
which wants to help and save man through Jesus
(cf. Mk 2:5 ff). It does, of course, imply at least
a trace of the conviction that Jesus is the expected messiah; but Jesus does not appear to
expect a clear profession to that effect. He does
not demand too much of men; when a distressed
heart turns to him and trusts in him for help
and healing, the understanding will come of itself
(cf. Mk 7:37).

Of his disciples, Jesus expects that his nearness
will give them the certainty of God's protection.
Thus he upbraids them in the storm: "Why are
you so fearful? Have you no faith?" (Mk 4:40).
Their failure lies in their lack of confidence, their
"little faith" according to Matthew (cf. Mt 8:26;
14:31; 16:8; and Lk 12:28). Mark, who often
blames the disciples for lack of understanding,
and even for their hard hearts (Mk 6:52; 7:18;
8:17), interprets their failure as fundamentally
a failure to understand Jesus' personality (cf.
4:41), and makes it quite clear to his readers that
to have faith means also to have gained the certainty that Jesus is the son of God. But ultimately, that is possible only after his resurrection.
According to Matthew, the disciples make this
profession of faith already after Jesus walked on
the water (14:33; see also 16:16 for Peter's confession). The examples of "great faith" which he

offers to his readers are the pagan captain (8:10), and the Canaanite woman, also a pagan (15:28).

Jesus expects the faithful to believe that things impossible to human beings are possible by God's power (cf. Mk 9:23; 11:23 f.). Faith is assumed to have charismatic power: a faith no larger than a mustard seed can move mountains (Mt 17:20; cf. Lk 17:6). Such a faith, which leaves the theologians mostly helpless, is Jesus' great concern, and he assigns to it a special place in prayer (cf. Mt 11:24). There is no doubt, no hesitation—God will grant the petition.

Yet it would be wrong to regard this faith which Jesus expects as something purely irrational. There is danger in a charismatic-enthusiastic piety which would do without the light of any theological reflection. But, as we said earlier, even in the synoptic gospels faith always presupposes at least the beginning of an intimation of Jesus' secret, a turning to this divine emissary, and a readiness to learn and ultimately to make a full confession of faith.

The witness of John's gospel is especially important in this context. It places the greatest emphasis on the confession of Jesus as the messiah and son of God—at times in formulations which clearly show the interest of the Church later on. (Cf. Jn 1:49; 4:42; 6:69; 9:25 f; 11:27; 16:27 f.; 20:28) The early Church understood Jesus' ministry to mean that he desired to be recognized and accepted as in a unique sense the bearer of salvation; and this understanding is expressed with greater emphasis in the gospel of John. Rightly, no doubt, for such certainly was Jesus' intention, although for the moment he contented himself with a faith not yet clarified—but nonetheless he wanted recognition of the things that came to pass through him, and also of the things which he, although at first in a secret and hidden manner, said about himself.

Our present concept of faith, clarified through dogma, is thus justified—and there is always good reason to clarify the content of faith. But it may be that we often use a wrong psychology of faith, and fail to lay our stresses properly. Men cannot live by a dessicated confession, clear as it may be—their faith cannot take on life that way. First of all, a man's entire being must be seized by the reality and power of faith, he must take his stand with God, he must have found his one and all in Christ—and from then on he will be open and accessible for a deepening and clarification of this faith. For to have faith does indeed mean to take a risk: the faithful always encounters new and often difficult problems that demand solution, to an extent solution by means of reason. But what allows a Christian to bear up and remain steadfast is ultimately not a faith of reason, but that profound tie to God and Christ which we can see in the Bible.

Let us take just one of the examples of faith from the gospel of John. Martha stands heartbroken at her brother's grave, and her faith in Jesus, too, is put to the test. It is unlikely that she fully understood the revelation in the Lord's words (Jn 11:25: f.). But when Jesus asks her "Do you believe this?" she answers with a full confession of faith in him, the Christ and son of God, who is to come into the world (11:27). The confession may be formulated in John's style and adapted to his readership (cf. 20:31), but there is no need to doubt the historical accuracy of Martha's response. We see here how faith overcomes darkness with another resource than intellectual understanding or reflection, although there is no lack of thought, and that resource is the profound and total allegiance to the person of Christ, with a steadfastness which in the last analysis is given by God's grace (cf. 6:44, 65). The other confessions in John's gospel, too, are of a similar character, including that of Thomas to the resurrected Christ. This disciple, inescapably identified with the byword "doubting," makes a confession that goes far beyond a mere conclusion drawn from his experience—a highly personal confession which is the high-point of the gospel report: "My Lord and my God!" (20:28). And the readers are taught this lesson, that faith should not ask for visible proof (20:29), but rely on testimony (20:30 f.).

Here is the best answer to a call for rational elucidation and demonstration of faith: we have the *testimony* of those who first accepted and proclaimed the faith in Christ. The apostolic witness offers himself in guarantee of the truth of his report, but in the nature of his testimony he can never give evidence or final certainty.

Once we have grasped this idea of testimony—
which shows itself already in Peter's speeches in
the Acts, and comes to full maturity in John[9]—
we shall not demand complete rational assurance
for our faith, and yet regard that faith as sufficiently rational and assured. Between the "blind
leap" and rational certainty there is the truth of
a genuine attitude of faith. The entire faith rests
on this foundation that God, by the testimony of
the apostles, has wakened Jesus from the dead;
this is the faith which unfolds in the christological confession.[10]

As we have seen, faith as faithful conduct has
in the New Testament, too, much of the character
of trust and confidence, of personal tie and total
allegiance. And this relation now applies no
longer only to God but also, and primarily, to
Jesus Christ. "Without having seen him you love
him; though you do not now see him you believe

---

[9] Cf. H. Strathmann in *ThWNT* IV (Stuttgart, 1942),
492–508; N. Brox, *Zeuge und Märtyrer* (Munich,
1961), 43–92; R. Schnackenburg, *Die Johannesbriefe*
(Freiburg i.Br., 1963), 52–58. On the theological
significance of the idea of the witness, see J. R.
Geiselmann, *Jesus der Christus* (Stuttgart, 1951),
31–48.

[10] Geiselmann, *loc. cit.*, speaks of the paradosis of the
apostles of Jesus as the Christ (54–101) and explicates its content (104–130). Among Protestants,
W. Pannenburg attempts to understand all Christology in terms of Jesus' resurrection: *Grundzüge
der Christologie* (Gütersloh, 1964), esp. pp. 47–112.

in him and rejoice with unutterable and exalted joy . . ." (1 Peter 1:8). The true faith in Christ implies an inner urge to personal surrender, to follow the exalted Lord.

There is much more to be learned from the New Testament about faith; but what we have said may suffice to lay stress once again, in the light of the Bible, on certain aspects which we have perhaps tended to overlook and to underrate: to take one's stand with God who brings the dead alive; to submit in trust and obedience; to wait and hope in loyalty; and finally the personal allegiance to Christ, the total self-surrender to him who is for us "the true God and eternal life" (1 Jn 5:20), in the firm conviction that "I know whom I have believed" (2 Tim 1:12).

THE LIFE OF FAITH

It follows from what has been said that we cannot think of faith as one single act which leads to a perfect and complete condition, but rather as a living relationship into which we have entered with God and with Christ—a relationship that has to be carefully nursed, deepened, and intensified from here on. Faith is at times likened to a plant that must be cared for and protected. But the statements in the Bible, according to which faith is man's answer to God's revelation, and makes man God's partner, would suggest rather that faith is like a friendship: we must devote ourselves to our friend, take care of our friendship

and deepen it; for the relationship will be subject
to strains, to test and trial, and must hold or fall
apart. Only such a growing and ripening relationship with Christ and God allows us to taste the
whole joy of faith, and proves the power of faith
for Christian existence in this world. Then we are
"rooted and built up in him and established in the
faith, just as you were taught, abounding in thanksgiving" (1 Col 2:7).

The Bible has much to say on the growth and
life of faith, and on its dangers and trials. Chapter 11 of the Letter to the Hebrews contains a
collection of examples from the Old Testament
which the author of the Letter has probably
taken over from an earlier source.[11] Both the Jews
and the early Christians have learned from the
great man of faith. The "cloud of witness" in
Hebrews 11 begins with Abel, who "by faith
offered to God a more acceptable sacrifice than
Cain" (11:4); there follow Enoch and Noah, and
Abraham whose obedient migration to a foreign
land is like a symbol of faith,[12] as is his own and

---

[11] Cf. E. Stauffer, *New Testament Theology* (London,
1955); O. Michel, "Der Brief an die Hebräer" in
H. A. W. Meyer's *Commentary VIII* (Göttingen,
1949), 244 f.

[12] Abraham's entire wanderings, his being a stranger
in strange lands, his living in tents become a "symbol
of a more profound migration involving all existence": O. Kuss, *Der Brief an die Hebräer* (Regensburg, 1966), 172. Philo of Alexandria, in his *De
migratione Abrahami* (On Abraham's migration),

his descendants' dwelling in tents: "These all died in faith, not having received what was promised, but having seen it and greeted it from afar, and having acknowledged that they were strangers and exiles on the earth" (11:13). The passage clearly shows the underlying concept of faith of the Letter to the Hebrews: the firm anticipation of the invisible promises, the hope which makes future realization a certainty. It is a faith which has to meet the test of the world's darkness and conflicts. Even the trial of Abraham, so familiar to us, when he is told to sacrifice his own son, is mentioned in this context, and again we read: "He considered that God was able to raise men even from the dead" (v. 19). Nor have Isaac, Jacob, and Joseph been forgotten; the blessing at Jacob's deathbed is mentioned specifically (vv. 20–22). Next follows Moses who "by faith left Egypt, not being afraid of the anger of the king; for he endured as seeing him who is invisible" (v. 27). Israel's entire history is so full of examples that our author nearly loses his breath: "And what more shall I say? For time would fail me to tell of Gideon, Barak, Samson, Jephthah,

has given a different interpretation of Abraham's departure from his home for the land promised by God: Abraham departs from corporeal matters, from the perceptions of the senses and human discourse, and attains the knowledge of God and supreme union with him. By his allegory, Philo thus raised Abraham's way to be the exemplary type of what is human: the soul seeking God.

85

and David and Samuel and the prophets—who through faith conquered kingdoms, enforced justice, received promises, stopped the mouths of lions, quenched raging fires, escaped the edge of the sword, won strength out of weakness, became mighty in war, put foreign armies to flight . . ." (vv. 32–34). What all these paradigms have in common is this, that man's faith must be tested in trials and tribulations, and must be found true and obedient to God's call and command—and all this in a darkness that is inherent in the earthly station of the believer, in his status as *viator*. In their capacity merely as human beings, these righteous men of the Old Testament enjoy no wisdom greater than that of their contemporaries, but "through faith" they affirm God's promises, and seize the future as something real and certain. If men like these, who "did not receive what was promised" (v. 39), achieved all this, it behooves us all the more to "lay aside every weight, and sin which clings so closely, and let us run with perseverance the race that is set before us, looking to Jesus the pioneer and perfecter of our faith, who for the joy that was set before him endured the cross, despising the shame, and is seated at the right hand of the throne of God" (Heb 12:1). There is no doubt: faith must meet test and trial, faith is a race, a contest, and reaches maturity only in the imitation of Christ.

It is this aspect of faith, as a state of mind secure in divine grace and yet placed amidst the insecurities of the world, to which we should give greater thought in our present age; for to this tension are due the violent fluctuations of the life of faith. Faith in the sense of the New Testament means the conscious reaffirmation of faith, constantly put to the test, the alertness to God's call in the changing situations of life, and the responsible development of one's faith by self-examinination, prayer, and the effort to gain greater firmness of faith. Faith, too, can wither and die. Paul says about Abraham: "He did not weaken in faith when he considered his own body, which was as good as dead. . . . No distrust made him waver concerning the promise of God, but he grew strong in his faith as he gave glory to God, fully convinced that God was able to do what he had promised" (Rom 4:19 ff.). Faith is forever in motion, and may grow weaker or stronger; nothing endangers faith as much as a lazy peace.

The gospel according to John offers much material to study the growth and life of faith, its tests and trials, and also its decay and submergence in unbelief. Chapter 4, on Jesus' stay in Samaria, gives an example of how Jesus awakens faith and raises it to the level of a full confession. The evangelist does not intend to describe Jesus' encounter with the woman at Jacob's well in order to depict a masterpiece of spiritual guidance; on the contrary, he wants to show how Jesus, by revealing himself ever more clearly, awakens faith in the Samarian woman and eventually in her people as well. One can still recognize the several steps along the way that lead to

the acceptance of the Savior of the world (v. 42):
first it is "you, a Jew" (v. 9), then "Sir" (v. 11),
"are you greater than our father Jacob?" (v. 12),
"you are a prophet" (v. 19), and then "Can this
be the Christ?" (v. 29). The evangelist is even
more concerned to show that Jesus awakens faith
by his mere presence; in the end, the people of
Sychar say to the woman who brought them the
first news: "It is no longer because of your words
that we believe, for we have heard for ourselves,
and we know that this is indeed the Savior of the
world" (v. 42). Where there is the willingness to
listen to the bearer of the revelation, faith is not
far behind, even among the half-pagan Samaritans.

The theme of faith is carried further in the tale
of the official which immediately follows. To this
official, and to the Galileans who saw his miracles
in Jerusalem, Jesus says: "Unless you see signs
and wonders you will not believe" (4:48). Perhaps the evangelist has on purpose inserted these
words in a report of healing at a distance which
he took over from another source.[13] He wants to
give a lesson on faith to his readers: a mere faith

[13] Cf. R. Schnackenburg, "Zur Traditionsgeschichte
von Joh 4, 46–54," in *Biblische Zeitschrift* 8 (1964),
58–88. The word is of fundamental importance not
only for the evangelist's view of miracles, but for
faith in general. The man who wants to achieve faith
only by outward signs, and make sure of his faith
by tangible proof, fails to understand the true attitude of faith.

in miracles is not enough (cf. 2:23 ff.; 4:45), a search for thrills does not lead men to faith. In the situation here described, the faith of the anguished father is tested by the word. First, he asks more urgently: "Sir, come down before my child dies!" But after Jesus tells him: "Go; your son will live," the gospel continues: "The man believed the word that Jesus spoke to him and went his way" (4:50). Faith on the strength of the word alone is more than faith on the strength of signs and wonders. The official has inwardly grown; he has passed the test. His faith is rewarded when his servants come to meet him with the news that the fever left his son at the same hour when Jesus had spoken those words. The evangelist goes on to report that the official himself and his whole household believed—and that they believed fully in Jesus the Messiah. Thus Jesus leads this man to the decision; and the single act of faith has become a permanent attitude of faith. Each man, no doubt, must at some time make this conscious decision to believe, in his own personal manner; only then does faith turn into a firm inner possession.

But that possession will not remain unchallenged! The disciples in John's gospel serve to make that clear. All of them have made the decision to join Jesus. The evangelist tells vividly how the first disciples, pupils of John the Baptist, came to follow Jesus (1:35–51); and he gives special attention to the "conversion" of Nathanael who, though initially a skeptic enthusiastically confesses Jesus after their encounter (1:49). Still, the disciples' faith, its growth, its difficulties and its trials (cf. 6:66–71; 11:8–16), the disciples inability to comprehend together with their desire to believe[14]—all this remains the evangelist's theme right to the scene of the last supper. The reader feels how even these faithful men struggle to keep the faith, how unenlightened they are and yet how zealous; and we delight to read that Jesus recognized their faith nonetheless (cf. 6:70; 17:6 ff.). This faith of the disciples is a gift of grace, but even so it is also the fruit of their endeavor to accept and retain Jesus' words.[15] What keeps them by Jesus' side when most of his followers leave is a deep personal tie to him ("Lord, to whom shall we go?"), and the conviction that Jesus has "the words of eternal life," even though they do not yet understand them (6:68). Jesus himself is the pedagogue of their faith; he admonishes and helps them to believe, but also warns them against human cleverness, against a feeling of security (cf. 13:38; 16:31 f.), and gives them words of reassurance to help them in the coming times of trouble (cf. 13:19; 14:29; 15:18 ff.; 16:1 ff.).

All this the evangelist reports with the faithful of the future in mind—his own communities in which faith was encountering a number of problems. John's first letter shows this concern even

[14] Cf. Jn 13:6–9; 14:4–11; 16:16 ff., 29 ff.
[15] Cf. Jn 6:44 f., 70; 16:27; 17:8.

more clearly. A seductive heresy is being preached, an enthusiastic gnosis which promises man that he shall "have God" without a moral effort; the writer of the letter warns his addressees to hold fast to "what you heard from the beginning" (2:24), to keep the old and ever new commandment to love one another (2:7–11; 3:11). But problems arise not just from false ideologies but also from the success of pseudoprophets and the depressing knowledge that the faithful are in the minority.

The New Testament even knows the problem of faith growing lax, the problem of fatigue and lukewarmness. The Letter to the Hebrews is one single admonition to overcome the weakness, to "lift your drooping hands and strengthen your weak knees" (12:12). In the messages in the Apocalypse to the seven communities of Asia Minor, we read sharp reproof and earnest admonition. The message to the Laodiceans sounds as if it were addressed to our day: "Would that you were cold or hot! So, because you are lukewarm, and neither cold nor hot, I will spew you out of my mouth. For you say, I am rich, I have prospered, and I need nothing; not knowing that you are wretched, pitiable, poor, blind, and naked. Therefore I counsel you to buy from me gold refined by fire . . ." (Rev 3:16 ff.). The early Church is called to a faith of the saints: "If any one is to be taken captive, to captivity he goes; if any one slays with the sword, with the sword

91

must he be slain. Here is a call for the endurance and faith of the saints" (Ap 13:10).

Only where the faith remains alive, where it affirms itself in ever new decisions and gathers strength through personal experience, only there can it remain steadfast in the face of severe demands. The reciting of formulations of the creed, drill in memorizing the commandments, the appeal to the common bond of the Church, even vast manifestations have only limited value. We sense it on all sides that Christians today are inwardly in a *diaspora*;[16] the wastelands of unbelief, indifference, and godlessness are spreading. The walls of an externalized lip-service faith are collapsing or crumbling. Only where the clear fountain of a personal faith wells up, only there materialism and atheism are defeated.

UNBELIEF

Anyone trying to understand the nature of faith will do well to give thought to unbelief also; just as the meaning of "good" can be understood only after we have encountered sin and evil.

Scripture has a good deal to tell us about unbelief. But since a theoretical denial of God's existence is unknown to Scripture, "unbelief" there

[16] Cf. K. Rahner, "Theologische Deutung der Position des Christen in der modernen Welt," in *Sendung und Gnade* (Innsbruck, 1959), 13–47; R. Schnackenburg, "Gottes Volk in der Zerstreuung," in *Lebendiges Zeugnis* 1966, 2–4, pp. 18–31.

means something totally different from what it means today.[17] We have seen that Israel sinned by failing to trust in the God of the covenant, and by murmuring and disobedience (Ps 78 and 106). And there is still another form of unbelief. "The fool says in his heart, 'There is no God'" (Ps 14:1; 53:2); it means that he denies God's power in the world and feels contempt for God's punishment. Thus the author of the psalm continues: "They are corrupt, they do abominable deeds, there is none that does good." Unbelief is a rejection of God, not just in thought but even more in deed, a defiance of God and scorn for his law. The devout psalmist answers the unbelievers: "They shall be in great terror, for God is with the generation of the righteous" (Ps 14:5). Even in the Old Testament, such unbelief is felt to be a fearsome, evil power drawing man along to his

---

[17] Not until hellenistic times does Judaism have to struggle with the problem of atheism. It attempts to show God's existence, his power and glory, by the fact of creation (cf. Wisdom 13:1–9); the main polemic continues to be directed against "foolish" idol-worship (*ibid.*, 13:10; 14:20). "Knowledge of God" always meant to the Jews that God was to be acknowledged and revered in practice. In the Aristeas Letter 195, it is praised as the highest knowledge "that God rules all things" and "in his power he guides and accomplishes all things." The very same attitude shows itself in Paul, Rom 1:19–23. Concerning denial of God in the Scriptures, cf. J. Schmid in *LThK* IV (Freiburg i.Br., 1960), 1124 ff.

destruction—something dark and incomprehensible, a *mysterium iniquitatis*.

In the New Testament, which echoes with the Good Tidings, the message of God's joy and salvation, unbelief appears still more disastrous, the worst possible thing. Those men who close their hearts to God's final offer of salvation are in danger of the eschatological judgment. In Jesus' own sermons, such is the terrifying counterpart to his loving efforts to save his people. When the people demanded a sign from heaven, he recognized the voice of unbelief. "This generation," he said, "is an evil generation; it seeks a sign, but no sign shall be given except the sign of Jonah" (Lk 11:29), which means the justification of God's anointed at the *parousia*, when it is too late for repentance.[18] Elsewhere Jesus sighs: "O faithless and perverse generation, how long am I to be with you and bear with you?" (Lk 9:41). "Whoever is ashamed of Jesus and his words in this adulterous and sinful generation, of him will the Son of man also be ashamed when he comes in the glory of Father with the holy angels" (Mk 8:38). Jesus' experiences with his contemporaries, the Israelites of his day who were called to inherit his salvation, have made his judgment of them dark and melancholy. "Woe to you," he cries out over the three towns of Galilee who had

---

[18] Cf. A. Vögtle, "Der Spruch vom Jonaszeichen," in *Synoptische Studien (Festschrift für A. Wikenhauser)* (Munich, 1954), 230–277.

seen more of his mighty works than any others (Mt 11:20–24), and in a symbolic way curses the fig tree that bears no fruit (Mk 11:13 f).[19] Faith brings repentance and a return to God; but precisely those who should have been most receptive for this call of God, precisely they have failed. Jesus accuses the Pharisees and leaders of the people: "Truly I say to you, the tax collectors and the harlots go into the kingdom of God before you. For John came to you in the way of righteousness, and you did not believe him, but the tax collectors and the harlots believed him; and even when you saw, you did not afterward repent and believe him" (Mt 21:31 f.). All these things show the seriousness of the situation; with the coming of Jesus, who announces God's mercy and salvation for all mankind, each man is faced with the decision whether to repent and accept Jesus' message. Man must choose between faith and unbelief; there is no hiding place, no shirking, no flight into non-commitment. Those who do not believe will be lost and sink into unbelief.

But while the word of grace resounds, there remain possibilities to repent and return. In the

[19] This remarkable act will have to be understood as a prophetic, symbolic deed suggesting the beginning of the rejection of Israel. On this much discussed pericope, see especially J. W. Doeve, "Purification du Temple et dessèchement du figuier," in *New Testament Studies* 1 (1954/55), 297–308; G. Munderlein, "Die Verfluchung des Feigenbaums," *ibid.*, 10 (1963/64), 88–104.

gospel of John, where unbelief seems to be hanging over "the Jews," especially their leaders, like a cloud of disaster,[20] Jesus raises his beckoning call to the very last: "Walk while you have the light, lest the darkness overtake you; he who walks in the darkness does not know where he goes. While you have the light, believe in the light, that you may become sons of light" (12:35 f.). Even after Jesus has been condemned and crucified, the sermons of the apostles offer the Jews once more the opportunity to repent. Peter says: "Repent therefore, and turn again, that your sins may be blotted out, that times of refreshing may come from the presence of the Lord, and that he may send the Christ appointed for you, Jesus!" (Acts 3:19 f.). Today again, this call for repentance and return needs to be addressed to a mankind that has turned its back on God. When salvation is at stake, man must face the seriousness of the situation; he must be made aware that the only alternative left to him is faith or unbelief.

There are of course degrees of unbelief; John's gospel offers clear examples. The crowds who follow Jesus because of the miracles he performs on the sick, they are not yet unbelievers. Jesus feeds and fills the crowds; but then comes the crisis. His demand for complete faith in him, who

---

[20] A. Charue, *L'incredulité des Juifs dans le Nouveau Testament* (Gembloux, 1929); J. Jocz, "Die Juden im Johannesevangelium," in *Judaica* 9 (1953), 129–142; E. Grässer in *New Testament Studies,* 72–90.

was sent by God, who is the true bread of heaven and of life, reveals the unbelief of the Jews. They have judged his gifts superficially, and see in him only the carpenter's son; it now becomes manifest that there is no deep faith behind their affection, and soon the great desertion occurs (Chapter 6). This, too, must be stated openly—that a weak and half-hearted faith, a mere superficial "belonging," will be challenged sooner or later. When that crisis comes, it will leave either full and conscious faith, as among the Twelve, or open unbelief.

The Jewish leaders present a frightening example of what this unbelief is and where it leads. They do not stop at rejecting Jesus, merely shrugging him off. Once men refuse the offer of God's love, their hearts will harden and drive them to hatred, malice, and hostility. Jesus says of such men: "If I had not come and spoken to them, they would not have sin. . . . If I had not done among them the works which no one else did, they would not have sin; but now they have seen and hated both me and my Father. It is to fulfill the word that is written in their law, 'They hated me without a cause'" (15:22–25).

This fully developed, malicious, active, and hostile unbelief is in Jesus' view the mark of the God-despising world which remains under the influence of Satan. This unbelief is sin itself, of which the Holy Spirit will convict the world (Jn 16:8 f.). How will the Holy Spirit do so? The answer can only be: through the Church, which exposes unbelief in all its godlessness and evil, by virtue of her faith, even by her mere existence as a community of the faithful, and ultimately by her proclamation of salvation. This extreme view of unbelief as sin itself, of the mystery of evil that is at work in the sons of perdition (cf. 2 Thess 2:7; Eph 2:2), also throws light once again on the nature of faith: Faith is at root a belonging to God, as John says, a "being-from-God," and allegiance to Christ, the Son of God. Faith in the true and fullest sense, what Paul calls "faith working through love" (Gal 5:6), is present only where the sincerity of God's children, their existence filled with God's light and love and their consequent love for one another, becomes visible and effective.

We thus see faith to be a mighty challenge which we have never fully met and yet must try to meet more and more in the shifting context of history and the human condition: a total self-surrender to God and Christ, an acceptance of God and his revelation in Christ, unconditional trust in him and full reliance on his goodness and his promises, submission to his will, obedience, and a love like that with which he loved us. But our faith does not remain unchallenged and secure; we must forever struggle to maintain it, grow in it and be watchful. To do so, we must pray ever more ardently for faith: "Lord, increase our faith!" (Lk 17:5). In the full knowledge of our weakness, and yet always prepared and trusting, we may cry out: "I believe; help my unbelief!" (Mk 9:24).

IV

The Imitation of Christ

In recent years, in the course of the violent debate about "the historical Jesus" and "the Christ of faith," it has become clear that Jesus' call to follow and imitate him represents an original expression, and raises a unique, special, and until then unheard-of demand.[1] For with his call to follow him he establishes a unique relation between himself and those he calls, which in the New Testament is consistently called "discipleship," "a relation *sui generis*" determined exclusively by Jesus' own person. "Just as he himself has the final decision who may join his disciples, just so he alone gives form and content to this

[1] Cf. N. A. Dahl, "Der historische Jesus als geschichtswissenschaftliches und theologisches Problem," *Kerygma und Dogma* 1 (1953), especially 114–122; the symposium *Der historische Jesus und der kerygmatische Christus*, ed. H. Ristow and K. Matthiae (Berlin, 1960); F. Mussner, "Der historische Jesus" in *Der historische Jesus und der Christus unseres*

relation with his disciples."[2] None of the existing forms of discipleship among the Jews of that day —whether the relation of the students of the rabbis' school to their teachers, the relation of John's followers to the great baptizer at the Jordan, or the membership in the community of Qumran (who revered their "teachers of justice")—none of them begin to approach what Jesus intends and demands when he says to individual men: "Follow me!" It goes without saying that no comparison is possible between Jesus' demands and

Glaubens, ed. K. Schubert (Vienna, 1962), 103–128; H. Schürmann, "Der Jüngerkreis Jesu als Zeichen für Israel," *Geist und Leben* 36 (1961), 23–35; E. Schweizer, *Erniedrigung und Erhöhung bei Jesus und seinen Nachfolgern* (Zurich, 1962), 7–21. The Jewish historian of religion H. J. Schoeps, in an essay "Von der Imitatio Dei zur Nachfolge Christi," published in *Aus frühchristlicher Zeit* (Tübingen, 1950), pp. 286–301, writes: "There is hardly any other possibility than to start with his consciousness of being the Messiah, which allowed him to connect the demand of *imitatio dei* with the followership of his own person. . . . It would be more in harmony with the Jewish understanding of the Messiah to assume that Jesus, in his consciousness of being the Messiah, knew himself as the executor of the divine will, and called men to join him, his person, in order to follow God" (p. 291).

[2] Cf. K. H. Rengstorf, in *ThWNT* IV (Stuttgart, 1942), 37–45. The entire article on μαζητής is basic for the understanding of discipleship (pp. 417–465).

the decision to join a Hellenistic philosopher's school, be initiated in Hermetic gnostic teachings, or become an adept in a mystery cult. Jesus' call establishes a unique relationship with his disciples, in which Jesus is in all respects the master and the leader.[3]

Are we Christians of the present day still fully aware of what Jesus meant when he called men to follow him? Do we still have the same profound understanding for it as did the early Church, do we regard ourselves the "disciples" and followers of Christ in the same way as did the early Christians? Like so many other luminous words, the "imitation of Christ" has become a pale and shop-worn concept, covered with the dust of centuries and worn down by habituation. Not a few of today's Christians will think of Thomas à Kempis' little book when they hear the words—a book that may seem indispensable to some older and riper men as a guide to Christian living and source of spiritual refreshment, while others would throw it on the discard heap of obsolete ascetic

[3] Literature on the idea of imitation: G. Kittel in *ThWNT* I, 210–216; K. H. Schelkle, *Discipleship and Priesthood* (New York, 1965); H. Schürmann, *loc. cit.*; R. Schnackenburg, *The Moral Teaching of the New Testament* (New York, 1965); E. Neuhäusler, *Anspruch und Antwort Gottes* (Düsseldorf, 1962), 186–214; A. Schulz, *Nachfolgen und Nachahmen* (Munich, 1962), with further references; H. Zimmermann, "Christus nachfolgen," *Theologie und Glaube* 53 (1963), 241–255.

literature. Let us attempt, then, aided by the texts of the New Testament, to return that tarnished currency to its former splendor, to draw from the old instrument of Christian revelation once again the pure, full and bitter-sweet sounds that we hear in the New Testament. In this attempt, we shall, first, determine the original meaning of "imitation" in Jesus' own statements, second, investigate the meaning which the early Church gave to it after the crucifixion and the resurrection, and, third, try to apply our findings to today's situation and message.

THE ORIGINAL MEANING IN JESUS' OWN STATEMENTS

What sense Jesus himself attached to the term "imitation" has been recorded in the reports of how he called his disciples, even though these reports already exhibit a stylized, typical form. Jesus calls the brothers Simon and Andrew at Lake Genesareth with these words: "Follow me and I will make you fishers of men" (Mk 1:17). To "follow" thus means at first literally to walk after Jesus, accompany him on his way, be witnesses to his work, and help him with his tasks. Jesus wants to win men, and these disciples whom he has called, everyday professional fishermen, are to become fishers of men.[4]

[4] On this image, cf. O. Betz, "Donnersöhne, Menschenfischer und der davidische Messias" in *Revue de Qumran* 3 (1961), 41–70, specifically 53–61.

The pericope which Mark purposely placed at the beginning of Jesus' public life (1:16–20) contains a whole theology of the "imitation of Jesus." Jesus initiates the action which focuses in three points: Jesus' eye catches sight of the men, and immediately he *calls* them to come to him. His call is God's call, and when God calls man cannot but follow. The burden of the call is the demand *to go and follow after Jesus.* Finally, he will make them *fishers of men.* This is Jesus' action, and the men whom he called respond by their exemplary conduct. Again, we can discern three focal moments: Simon and Andrew leave their nets *instantly.* Both pairs of brothers *leave* the work they had been doing so far, and James and John the sons of Zebedee also leave their father and their kinfolk. The negative aspect of the "departure"[5] is submerged in the positive one: they are allowed to follow *after* Jesus, to enter into his community. Thus Jesus' call has received the expected answer.

The event which Jesus was then kindling was an "ingathering movement": He intended to

[5] The expression ’αποτάδδεσζαι in Lk 14:33 is significant; it originally means "take leave" but here acquires the meaning "renounce all one's possessions." Cf. H. J. Degenhart, *Lukas, Evangelist der Armen* (Stuttgart, 1965), 110–112, who feels that the core of the statement is not the sale of all possessions but the "abandonment of his present livelihood and activities, in order to devote himself exclusively to the Lord's service." (p. 111 f.)

gather the people of God who, hearing his message, would enter the kingdom of God. All men were to hear his message of salvation, believe in it, and turn to God with all their soul. In fact, the synoptic gospels report frequently that large multitudes "followed him" (e.g., Mk 5:24; Mt 14:13; 19:2; 20:29; Lk 7:9). But we must make a distinction between this common and superficial usage of the word, and the special "followership," the imitation to which the disciples are called. They enter into a more intimate followership, marked by the following. First, they receive a special call from Jesus, the summons to become his disciples. Second, they are given the specific task to render active help to Jesus' ingathering movement. The clearest example is the mission of the twelve, reported in all three synoptic gospels (Mk 6:7–13; Lk 10:1–20). And third, they must meet special demands. We are not talking here only of the concrete instructions that Jesus gives them when he sends them out into the surrounding towns and villages (Mk 6:8 f.). Much more, he demands of them their whole life. They must be willing to leave possessions and family (Mk 10–28), overcome all ambition and desire for fame and power (Mk 9:33 ff.; 10:42–45), and must even be prepared to lose their lives for his sake (Mk 8:34 f.). Jesus' "school of disciples" is less a house of learning than a hard and yet inspiring education.[6]

---

[6] There is no Jewish parallel for the imitation of Christ's suffering; but the idea of the suffering of the

While the early Church applied Jesus' demand to follow him to all the faithful, as we shall see, it will serve us nonetheless to keep the original, concrete meaning clearly in mind. The disciples are to give allegiance to the person of Jesus—the Jesus walking on this earth; they are to share his life, to live with him in his community, collaborate in his gathering of a people of God during the final days of the world, and walk his way with him as God designs it. The somewhat confusing fact that Jesus called some men to leave their house and home, while leaving others free to stay, might be understood in this way: concerning assignments in the outer world, Jesus distinguished among men according to their fitness and

just, and the vicarious atonement of the martyrs, is very much alive. Cf. E. Schweizer, *loc. cit.*, 21–33; E. Lohse, *Märtyrer und Gottesknecht* (Göttingen, 1955). What is distinctive in Jesus' attitude is that he binds his disciples to follow like him along the way which he saw before him as divinely ordained. No doubt the early Church underlined this matter in composing Mk 8:31–38, although basing itself on authentic sayings of Jesus. On Mk 8:35 and the words on losing one's life, cf. Dautzenberg, *Sein Leben bewahren* (Munich, 1966), 51–67; he writes justly: "Even if the ἕνεκεν ἐμοῦ of Mk 8:35 and Mt 10:39 is not part of the original formulation of the logion, the logion cannot be understood apart from the disciples' community with Jesus; the idea of the ἕνεκεν ἐμοῦ, even if not put into words, must have stood behind the call to make the decision" (60).

Christian Existence in the New Testament

abilities to perform certain tasks; but when it came to inward allegiance to him, he called upon all men who wished to enter God's kingdom. Here the decisive thing was the will to exist entirely for God's sake, to devote oneself undividedly to his service (Mt 6:24), to seek God's kingdom and to leave all else in God's hands (Lk 12:29 ff.). In his sermons to all the people, in the synagogues and at Lake Genesareth, in his Sermon on the Mount (Mt 5–7; Lk 6:20–49), and in his disputations with the scribes, Jesus in his divine mission proclaimed how God's will was to be done in these days when salvation was at hand. All men were to give answer to God's call in the hour of salvation;[7] but the special call of Jesus, to follow him and be his disciple, was addressed only to a few individuals. Yet anyone who rightly understood God's unconditional claim for the whole man, would have to be prepared, in principle, to follow also Jesus' special call (cf. Mk 10:17-21). It thus becomes understandable why the early Church applied to all the faithful many of Jesus' words which were no doubt originally addressed only to his disciples, thereby blurring the distinction between Jesus' "popular sermons" and his instructions to the disciples.[8]

[7] Cf. E. Neuhäusler, *loc. cit.*
[8] After Easter, the concept of discipleship is on occasion extended to all the faithful: thus, in Acts 6:21, this special usage becomes intelligible if one considers that the community with Jesus, and the loyalty to him, which remained effective for the

106

For example, Jesus' radical words: "If anyone comes to me and does not hate his own father and mother and wife and children and brothers and sisters, yes and even his own life, he cannot be my disciple"—no doubt these words had been originally addressed to those who are to leave everything for his sake and to become his closest followers. But the early Church interpreted the words to make their high demands on all those who join Jesus in faith; and thus we read in the introduction that Jesus was speaking to the "great multitudes" which accompanied him. Matthew clarifies the saying correctly: "He who loves father or mother more than me is not worthy of me" (Mt 10:37). The "disciples in the strict sense," then, those who are called to share constantly in Jesus' wanderings, occasionally to join in his proclamation, and to live in close community with him—they only demonstrate to a particularly high degree what it means to follow him; but this does not mean that all other men are therefore relieved of the same duties, the same tasks. The fact that the closer disciples are then given also special powers and offices need not be

original disciples even after the Lord's exaltation, must in a similar manner apply to those converted after Easter. Cf. K. H. Rengstorf in *ThWNT* IV, 462 f. An example for the intermingling of words originally addressed to the disciples, with instructions to the people at large, is the Sermon on the Mount; for the rest, cf. second section, below.

discussed in this context; here we are interested only in man's relation to Jesus, and the demands he makes on all who would enter God's kingdom. Thus the disciples' original relation to him is truly the archetype of what the "imitation of Christ" means: not—or not only and not primarily—the imitation of Jesus' character traits, not the emulation of his lofty example, but a personal allegiance to him, a listening to his word, a following on his way.

The point is made most clearly in the somewhat over-used words: "If any man would come after me, let him deny himself and take up his cross and follow me" (Mk 8:34). These words, which have come down to us with slight variations in more than one source, place the main emphasis on self-denial; the image of "taking up the cross," which the early Church surely understood to refer to Jesus' own cross, is used by Jesus himself still merely as a simile,[9] referring to the extreme consequence of self-denial: the readiness to lay down one's life (cf. Mk 8:35). It may be that the words "self-denial," which are absent in the parallel passage in Luke 14:27 (cf. Mt 10:38),

[9] Cf. E. Dinkler, "Jesu Wort vom Kreuztragen," *Neutestamentliche Studien für R. Bultmann* (Berlin, 1954), 111–129. His interpretation of the "cross" as the binding and protective *taw* sign, a penitential sign of God's faithful (esp. Ezra 9:4 ff.) is hardly tenable; cf. E. Schweizer, *loc. cit.*, 15. The logion is treated in more detail by A. Schulz, *loc. cit.* (note 3), 82–90.

are an addition to make this meaning clearer. What Jesus demands of his disciples is this: total renunciation of their own will, of honor, and of earthly happiness, in the painful-blessed companionship of wandering with Jesus on his way appointed to him by God. But they are not melancholy wanderers; before them shines Jesus' promise: "Every one who has left houses or brothers or sisters or father or mother or children or lands, for my name's sake, will receive a hundredfold, and inherit eternal life" (Mt 19:29). Even the early Church began to meditate on these words;[10] according to the original version, the hundredfold reward is eternal life. The wanderings, although strenuous at present, lead toward a glorious goal; Jesus' faithful companions through temptation and suffering will some day share also in his dominion and his glory. The twelve who stay with Jesus during his times of trial, receive his promise: "As my Father appointed a kingdom for me, so do I appoint for you" (Lk 22:28). The promise that they shall eat and drink at Jesus' table holds for all those who were his close companions on this earth; and the the early Church recalled these words when

---

[10] This is shown by the form in Mark (10:30), where a reward is held out even "now in this time"; the community is thus considered as Jesus' "family"; the reward, however, is still connected "with persecutions." Cf. J. Schmid, *Das Evangelium nach Markus* (Regensburg, 1954), 197 f.

celebrating the eucharist (cf. Lk 22:16–18).

The hard and unconditional character of the imitation of Christ is expressed in three statements of the Lord, recorded by Luke (9:57–62). To a man who offers himself as a follower, Jesus replies: "Foxes have holes, and birds of the air have nests; but the Son of man has nowhere to lay his head." The purpose of this scene is not to record an incident in the life of Jesus—as though Jesus wanted to scare this man off, only to call to himself another man in the next incident, who protests: "Let me first go and bury my father." Rather, what matters here are only Jesus' pronouncements which make clear the lofty and absolute demands he makes. To follow Jesus means to be prepared to endure the insecurity of life with him; for the Son of man has no home,[11] and offers nothing to those who follow him except communion with himself who is homeless. For his sake they are to ignore all other earthly duties, even the sacred duty of piety toward their parents. "Leave the dead to bury their own dead!" —a daring, even violent word which may possibly be based on a proverb: The man who is

---

[11] A number of exegetes here conjecture an original proverb which would have spoken of "man" only. In spite of a parallel in Plutarch, the hypothesis is rather improbable. The old tradition of the source of the saying (Mt 8:20) means by "the Son of man" Jesus, in an exclusive sense. This logion belongs to that group in which the words "Son of man" refer

called to do a more important service to the living may leave the civic duties to others. The proclamation of God's kingdom brooks no delay, allows no excuses. We here notice that Jesus can call men to leave the framework of respectability, the normal setting of human communal living. And finally, there is the third statement: "No one who puts his hand to the plow and looks back is fit for the kingdom of God!" These words, no doubt, apply primarily to those who proclaim the message, but at bottom they apply to all who would enter God's kingdom with Jesus.

Jesus' call to follow him is a claim to the entire man. The point can be made clear with the help of a passage whose exegesis and theology are disputed: Jesus' encounter with the rich young ruler (Mk 10:17–22). The passage plays an important role in the matter of the so-called evangelic counsels; we here present in brief only one interpretation.[12] Jesus' intention regarding this young man, who is an honest seeker striving for the kingdom of God, is single and unified from the outset. He wants to win him as a fol-

to Jesus in respect of his activity on earth; if the community had inserted the title only secondarily in an original saying of Jesus (adding "I"), there would have to be a reason. Cf. E. Tödt, *Der Menschensohn in der synoptischen Überlieferung* (Gütersloh, 1959), 114: "Jesus appears as he who has full authority to call men to follow him. The name 'Son of man' is used to designate his majesty, his authority."

[12] See also Chapter VI, below.

111

lower and thus lead him to God's kingdom. And so he does not offer him two ways—the "common" one of the Ten Comandments, and an "extraordinary" one of renunciation of his earthly goods. Rather, Jesus had discerned that it is his wealth which stands in the man's way to eternal life. Jesus perhaps means to point this out to the young man by his formulation of the commandments; in Mark's account, the commandments include the strange statement: "Do not defraud!" (10:19). Interpreted by Jewish parallels this may mean: "Do not withhold just wages!" Many exegetes are of the opinion that the statement is intended to combine the ninth and tenth commandments; but again the point would be the desire for earthly possessions. The ninth and tenth commandments "protect the neighbor's possessions, but most of all the possessions of the poor, against the 'greed' of others."[13] Be that as it may, according to Mark's gospel this much is clear: Jesus tells this man, who believes that he has observed the commandments from his youth: "You lack one thing; go, sell what you have, and give to the poor . . . and then come, follow me!" (Mk 10:21).

This case has a typical character. It is not typical in the sense that total poverty is demanded of all who aspire to membership in God's king-

[13] E. Lohmeyer, *Das Evangelium des Markus* (H. A. W. Meyer's *Kommentar*, I) (Göttingen, 1937), 210.

dom, although Jesus considers wealth one of the greatest dangers (cf. Mk 10:23–27).[14] But it is typical in the sense that Jesus lays claim to the whole man, and asks him to surrender precisely those things to which his heart is secretly most attached. "No one can serve two masters. . . . You cannot serve God and mammon" (Mt 6:24). Jesus' reply to the rich young ruler is not a commandment that is binding on all men, but summons this concrete human being to that specific form of followership which had found realization at that time in the group of Jesus' disciples. Yet the reply gives guidelines to each man, compelling him to consider what demands Jesus makes on him personally. Thus it applies not only to Jesus' disciples in the strict sense, to the evangelists and later priests and monks—it applies to every Christian; for every Christian is called to follow Christ in some form, even though his way of life cannot be the same as that of the disciples of that day. The imitation of Christ always demands concrete realization, whether we live in the world or in the cloister, whether we serve in the world as priests or as laymen.

[14] Cf. R. Schnackenburg, *The Moral Teaching of the New Testament* (New York, 1965); R. Völkl, *Christ und die Welt nach dem Neuen Testament* (Würzburg, 1961), 20–26; H. J. Degenhardt, *Lukas, Evangelist der Armen,* 136–153.

HOW THE EARLY CHURCH UNDERSTOOD
THE IMITATION OF CHRIST

As we have seen, the early Church applied Jesus' words about following him to all the faithful. There was the conviction that the transfigured Lord continued to be in communion with his own, not only with his original disciples but with all those who had become his "disciples" through faith. In Acts 6–21, all faithful are called "disciples." What Jesus had originally said only to his closest and most loyal followers, who had remained with him as his "little flock" (Lk 12:32), is now to be extended to all later believers. The evangelists often express this extension through incidental statements. Jesus' words about man taking up his cross and following him are placed in a group of sayings which open with "And he called to him the multitude with his disciples . . ." (8:34). Luke, in the corresponding passage (9:23), has it that Jesus spoke "to all," and then adds that man must take up his cross "daily." The imitation of Jesus must pass the test continuously, in everyday life. The audience of the Christian instruction now includes all the faithful and the catechumens. Today, we are beginning to see the gospels as textbooks and catechisms of the early Church. What they tell of Jesus' words and deeds is intended to enter into the lives of the Christians, and to bear fruit in every follower of Christ. It is no accident that the passage in which Jesus for the first time foretells his passion to his disciples is followed immediately by that series of sayings on the bearing of the cross, and saving and losing one's life, and on gaining the world while forfeiting life itself (Mk 8:34–38). It is further characteristic how Mark 10:29 extends the meaning of the saying about the hundredfold reward: such reward will be given even in this present life—and the evangelist here has in mind the brothers and sisters of the Christian community who constitute Jesus' new family (cf. Mk 3:34 f.). But there immediately follows the remark that such reward is connected "with persecutions." The full reward that is beckoning is the eternal life in the age to come.

The apostle John applies the idea of discipleship in his own way; he ties it closely to Jesus' call for faith. In John 8:12, Jesus speaks these graphic and memorable words: "I am the light of the world; he who follows me will not walk in darkness, but will have the light of life." The closely related passage 12:35 shows that to "follow" here means to believe in him; and the same image is further elaborated: "The light is with you for a little while longer. Walk while you have the light, lest the darkness overtake you; he who walks in the darkness does not know where he goes. While you have the light, believe in the light, that you may become sons of light." We obviously are no longer dealing with men walking after Jesus in the literal sense, but with a spiritual followership—with everything John means by "faith." There is a deep symbolism behind the expression: Jesus is the "light of the world," the revealer and giver of life, who has come from the heavenly world of light and life down into this darkened cosmos of death, and who will now take back up to heaven with him all those who join him. To "follow" him thus means ultimately to ascend in his footsteps up to the heavenly world. Christ leads the faithful through the darkness of this earthly world where man without Christ's guidance loses his way and is lost.

Nor are the synoptic words about followership absent from John's gospel. The words about losing one's life to save it have found a place in John 12:25, and are there followed by other words formulated in John's own spirit: "If anyone serves me, he must follow me; and where I am, there shall my servant be also" (12:26). For John, the way to the kingdom of heaven is through the cross. The Son of man is "exalted" in a twofold sense—by mounting the cross, and by going beyond it into heaven (cf. John 3:14; 8:28; 12:32). And those whom he draws after him must go the same way; they are summoned to follow him, and at the same time they are promised that they will be where he himself is. This thought finds clear expression in a dialogue with Simon Peter. At the last supper, the Lord says to Peter: "Where I am going you cannot follow me now; but you shall follow afterward" (13:36). In the epilogue, the resurrected Christ warns Peter of his martyrdom and asks him: "Follow me!" (21:18 f.). Jesus' disciple must submit to the will of the Father, who may lead him "where he does not wish to go."

A summons to follow Christ in his passion occurs also in 1 Peter 2:21 ff. The passage repeats, even elaborates, the old image—"you should follow in his steps." In this parenesis for the suppressed and suffering domestic slaves, another trait now comes to the fore: *imitation.*[15] Christ's own suffering in silence and obedience to God, after the example of the servant of Isaiah 53, becomes the model. Peter's letter is the classic statement of the *Imitatio Christi:* "Christ has left you an example, that you should follow in his steps. He committed no sin; no guile was found on his lips. When he was reviled, he did not revile in return; when he suffered, he did not threaten; but he trusted to him who judges justly." This admonition to the "passive virtues"—patience, meekness, and the unresisting readiness to suffer, or what is caustically called a slave mentality—may have discredited the imitation of Christ with many people. But the thought is merely the application of a much broader idea to a specific situation.

The element of imitation is already implied in the idea of followership. Jesus, exhorting his disciples to selfless service, refers them to his own example: "Whoever would be great among you must be your servant, and whoever would be first among you must be slave of all. For the Son of

[15] A. Schulz, *loc. cit.*, 176–179 and elsewhere, believes that Greek ethics, with its emphasis on example, accounts to some extent for this feature of imitation.

man also came not to be served but to serve . . ." (Mk 10:43 ff.). In John's report stress is laid on Jesus' humble service in washing the disciples' feet: "If I, then, your Lord and Teacher, have washed your feet, you also ought to wash one another's feet. For I have given you an example, that you also should do as I have done to you" (Jn 13:14 f.). The evangelist has in mind that the washing of the disciples' feet is a further sign foreboding the death on the cross—Jesus' supreme service of love (cf. Jn 13:1). 1 Jn 3:16 draws the consequences: "By this we know love, that he laid down his life for us; and we ought to lay down our lives for the brethren." The Lord's suffering and death, in which the disciple is to follow him, was in the early Church also seen as a paradigm.

In all these contexts, to "imitate" does not mean merely to copy, but always to join and follow. The "imitator" is always a follower. E. Schweizer[16] gives a striking example to make the matter clear: A sudden, heavy snowfall has cut off the child who has gone visiting. The father comes to fetch it and leads the way, making a path with his strong legs through the high snow-drifts. The child follows, step by step, putting its feet into the father's tracks. If the father wanted to be only a "model" to the child, the child would have to clear its own path alongside, merely imitating the father's way of doing it. In

[16] *Erniedrigung und Erhöhung,* 7.

118

the relation between the Christian and Christ, followership always remains the principal element—imitation is only a partial aspect.

A final, eloquent expression of the idea of followership is found in Ap 14:1–5. The prophet beholds the hundred and forty-four thousand who stand with the Lamb on Mount Zion—a symbol of the Church on earth, oppressed and in distress but yet protected by the Lord, as a comparison with Chapter 7 makes clear.[17] "These have been redeemed from mankind as first fruits for God and the Lamb," and "it is these who follow the Lamb wherever he goes" (14:4). They prove themselves worthy of being God's elect by following the Lamb obediently and faithfully. Above all, the author is thinking of steadfastness even to the point of martyrdom (cf. Jn 12:26; 13:36; 21:18; Ap 13:10). The "chastity" of the redeemed, "who have not defiled themselves with women," is a symbolic expression for their rejection of idolatry and emperor worship.[18] Thus they

[17] Cf. A. Wikenhauser, *Die Offenbarung des Johannes* (Regensburg, 1959), 111 f.; A. Schulz, *loc. cit.*, 170 f.
[18] Commentators are divided in their opinion. Most of the Fathers, many Catholic exegetes (É.-B. Allo, A. Gelin, E. Schick) as well as Protestant exegetes (E. Lohmeyer, J. Behm) insist on the literal meaning of "virginal" people. But there are opposing voices even on the Catholic side (A. Wikenhausen, M.-É. Boismard). The principal reason for the symbolic interpretation is that at this point the reference is to the entire people of God at the time of the eschaton.

are the ideal vision of the Church of the martyrs, bound in loyalty to its Lord. Even on earth, these followers of the Lamb hear the "new song," the song of redemption and victory sung by a heavenly choir, and only they can learn—that is, appropriate—that song (14:2 f.). Thus even in their tribulations they experience the certainty of Christ's triumph and their own salvation.

It may seem all the more surprising that one of the greatest theologians of the early Church, Paul, does not say one word about "following Christ." But though he does not know the concept, the thought is there, even in a form that is theologically far more profound. We recognize the thought as we listen to Paul's words on sharing in Christ's death and resurrection, his suffering and his transfiguration.[19] In Paul's eyes, the entire life of the Christian is life with Christ, indeed a fellowship and followership in Christ's death and resurrection. Such is the way of Christ, ordained by God, on which the Christian is to join his Lord. Membership among the followers of Christ is gained sacramentally in baptism; in Romans 6, Paul speaks of baptism into Christ's death and burial which will lead the Christian also to being

---

[19] Cf. E. Larsson, *Christus als Vorbild* (Uppsala, 1962). This author goes into the question how "followership" or "discipleship" is reflected in Pauline thought; he believes that the gospel statements on the matter were in some way known to the apostle (77 and passim) and influenced his theology (105).

united with him in a resurrection like his. And with it comes the moral duty to be dead to sin, and to live for God. The way through death to life with Christ, Paul is convinced, is the mark of Christian existence. Of daily suffering and distress, of which the apostle had to bear more than his share, he says "I die every day" (1 Cor 15:31). But through his union with Christ, these sufferings become for him the certainty of resurrection and of life: "We are always carrying in the body the death of Jesus, so that the life of Jesus may also be manifested in our bodies. For while we live we are always being given up to death for Jesus' sake, so that the life of Jesus may be manifested in our mortal flesh" (2 Cor 4:10 f.). Paul wants to know Christ and "the power of his resurrection, and share his sufferings, becoming like him in his death, that if possible I may attain the resurrection from the dead" (Phil 3:10 f.).

These thoughts have their roots deep in Pauline theology. To Paul, Christ is the second Adam, the father of new mankind, and his way is the way of all his brothers. His followers belong to him, they are united and beholden to him. "And those who belong to Christ Jesus have crucified the flesh with its passions and desires" (Gal 5:26). And they will also share with him, and through him, in the resurrection; for the day will come when Christ will conform them to the image of his glory (cf. Rom 8:29; 1 Cor 15:49; Phil 3:21).

In the light of Paul's vision, we can more clearly discern an aspect of followership which might otherwise be overlooked: We do not only follow after Christ, we are also closely united with him. We learn from Paul that we can follow Christ only within the Christian community, that to follow him is to realize that community in the Christian situation of today. We are still pilgrims (2 Cor 5:6 f.) and still struggling (2 Cor 10:3–6). Our new existence in Christ is still tied to the situation of this present age in which the power of evil is still free to operate (cf. Gal 1:4; Rom 8:35–39; Eph 6:12). Therefore we must undergo Christ's way with him: through the cross to resurrection, through suffering to glory.

APPLICATION TO THE CHRISTIAN SITUATION OF TODAY

The time has come to use the insights which we have gained from the New Testament texts, and draw from them some conclusions for the present world situation and kerygma.

a) The imitation of Christ is possible in the Christian community only by virtue of a deep, grace-given union with our Lord. We may not understand imitation of Christ primarily as a moral demand, or formulate it primarily as an ethical summons. Rather, the demand that we conform to Christ and follow him on his way even through suffering and tribulations and temptations, this demand is to grow out of the reality of our "being in Christ." This is the meaning also of the famous passage in Paul's Letter to the

Philippians, where an urgent call to unity, humility, and selflessness is followed by a mighty hymn to Christ, describing the way of Jesus Christ from his heavenly preexistence, through humiliation on earth, to eternal Lordship (2:6–11). And the transition is made by this little sentence: "Have this in mind among yourselves, which you have in Christ Jesus. . . ." (v. 5). The formulation "in Christ Jesus," occurs seven more times in this letter, in similar contexts, and no doubt points to the Christian's union with Christ, and their dependence on him. It probably means "as is proper for those who are united with Jesus Christ."[20] The hymn to Christ that follows does not present the Lord to the Philippians only or primarily as a model of character and convictions, but most of all as the forerunner and leader

---

[20] Cf. E. Käsemann, "Kritische Analyse von Phil 2:5–11," *Zeitschrift für Theologie und Kirche* 47 (1950), 313–360, giving a survey of the exegetical discussion (314–328) and a summarizing judgment (355 f.). Prevailing opinion since then vacillates between an "ethical" understanding and one oriented upon "life in Christ." An attempt to dissolve this alternative is G. Strecker, "Redaktion und Tradition im Christushymnus Phil 2," *Zeitschrift für die neutestamentliche Wissenschaft* 55 (1964), 63–78, specifically 66–68. According to him, the hymn carries an ethical stress, but on the basis that the community is constituted by the cross. The action of the *kyrios* that eventuates in the cross sets norms also for the ethical life of the community.

on a God-appointed way which they, too, must follow because they belong to him most closely, and because their performance in life is determined by him. Just as Christ went on his way in obedience to God, as a servant, just so the Christians must in their union with him follow this way and obey the law of selfless service. To do so, it is necessary to see the image of Christ in all its humanity and greatness, and to understand his personality in its unique significance for man's salvation. And it is necessary further to grasp our union with Christ in the depths of a personal faith. It must again become a reality that "Christ may dwell in our hearts through faith" (Eph 1:17).

b) Imitation of Christ, however, also means to follow one's own way in keeping with one's God-given vocation. God speaks to every man through the circumstances of his life, his earthly profession, social position, his family, and everything God gives to man as his "fate." The word is vague, but we can give it religious and Christian meaning: it is what God sends us, what he disposes for us. Every man feels that his "fate" is personal, that it concerns him above all, and that he must come to terms with it one way or another. The Christian faith is capable of endowing "fate" with meaning: it is to accept fate in imitation of Christ who, God's obedient servant, walked a way of unspeakable difficulty on earth, but saw the goal ahead, and attained it for our sake. In this way the imitation of Christ becomes a thought which pervades life, and helps us overcome life's difficulties.

c) What matters most in the example set for us by the Lord whom we follow is not to imitate specific qualities and attitudes, but to let him show us the direction, in the sense of John's words: "I am the light of the world; he who follows me will not walk in darkness, but will have the light of life" (Jn 8:12). Christ is the light of revelation piercing the darkness of confused opinions and confusing propaganda. He is the light of true life, the source of strength for meaningful existence, who transcends the fleeting life on this earth. He also is the light of joy and hope in times which, despite all their enjoyment and glitter, lack inner joy and true hope. A fundamental orientation to Christ, and to the view of world and life to which he guides us, is more important than any specific concrete instructions, any specific attitudes. Even so, Jesus Christ gives us the decisive answers to these problems, too, above all the one "new commandment" to love one another even as he has loved us (Jn 13:34; 15:12, 17).

d) A man who has so radically become a follower of Christ will not be frightened by Christ's radical demands. True, there are many tenets of our moral doctrine which modern man barely understands any longer, or receives with inner assent. We need think only of certain questions of sexual and marital morals. There is true distress here, not merely a distress due to modern living conditions and attitudes, but also a deeply human distress—ultimately a lack of faith. Only that Christian can meet it who, in the light of his faith in Christ, understands the meaning of Jesus' demands—demands intended to save him from his human condition, and unite him with the God of love and salvation. Only that Christian will not lose courage who, trusting in the Lord who leads the way, his Master and friend, continues on his own way step by step, weak and yet confident, stumbling and picking himself up; such a Christian knows the difficulties of his way in this world, and yet strives hopefully toward his goal.

e) At the end, there waits not the hard demand but the joyful tidings of the gospel. The imitation of Christ is the most glorious promise, and thus brings the profoundest joy even during the hardships of the way. Jesus did not reprove his disciples when Simon Peter reminded him that they had left everything to follow him; on the contrary he promises them a hundredfold reward and eternal life. Hope inspired the early Church to rejoice even in tribulations and tears, as we read in the First Letter of Peter: "In this [the eschatological end prepared for you] you rejoice, though now for a little while you may have to suffer various trials, so that the genuineness of your faith, more precious than gold which though perishable is tested by fire, may redound to praise and glorify and honor at the revelation of Jesus Christ. Without having seen him you love him; though you do not now see him you believe in him and rejoice with unutterable and exalted joy. As the outcome of your faith you obtain the salvation of your souls" (1 Peter 1:6–9).

Similar words are found in the Letter to the Hebrews: "Therefore, since we are surrounded by so great a cloud of witnesses (to faith), let us also lay aside every weight, and sin which clings so closely, and let us run with perseverance the race that is set before us, looking to Jesus the pioneer and perfecter of our faith, who for the joy that was set before him endured the cross, despising the shame, and is seated at the right hand at the throne of God" (12:1 f.).

V

The Sermon on the Mount and Modern Man

It speaks well for Christianity today that there is such a burning interest and honest search for Jesus' moral teaching. The shock of two world wars, social upheavals, a keener social sense, the ardent seeking for the meaning of human life that we witness in philosophy, art, and literature—these and other factors have made an old-style bourgeois morality impossible. Such a morality now seems like a Christian cloak which did not quite conceal the un-Christian immorality underneath. Much was rotten behind a fine facade. We need to recall only the social banishment of men who had violated the ruling moral code, or the exploitation of labor by allegedly Christian employers. Yet it would be a mistake to consider our time better, by virtue of its social institutions, than the time before World War I. The radical transformation of our style of life has brought with it a rejection of that bourgeois self-satisfied hypocrisy which has so discredited Christianity. Man today has again become more honest; he either

128

admits freely what we, as Christians, must call immoral, or else he is honestly troubled by the disharmony between the law of Christ and his own living conduct. There still are no doubt many routine Christians, who barely hide their lack of love for their fellowmen behind a Christian front. But there are also many who seriously want to know what Christianity means, who try to realize their faith and shoulder Christian responsibility in the world. Many older people feel oppressed by the demands of Christian morality, and not a few of the young would like to live according to the precepts of Christ, but fail because of their own weakness and the nearly insuperable resistance of the world around them. Man today is in no way better, but he has perhaps become more honest to God, and to himself.[1]

[1] Thus the title of the bestselling book by Bishop John A. Robinson, *Honest to God* (London, 1963); the book has stirred up world-wide discussion. Cf. among others, *Die religiöse Religionslosigkeit des Bischofs Robinson,* in *Evangelische Theologie* 24 (1964), 178–195; H. W. Augustin, Ed., *Diskussion zu Robinsons Gott ist anders* (Munich, 1964); (Cath.) E. Schillebeeckx, *Personale Begegnung mit Gott* (Mainz, 1964), and *Neues Glaubensverständnis* (Mainz, 1965). The discussion reveals modern man's radical resolve to reexamine his entire religious position, and to question even the faith in a transcendent, "objectively" existing God; it cannot be denied that often unclear philosophical and theological concepts are introduced. Besides, modern man is often mistaken in his views about what may still be consid-

In such a situation, Jesus' Sermon on the Mount becomes a problem for us. We may not hypocritically soften Jesus' words, nor can we brush them aside in fear; and yet the question troubles us: Can we meet these extreme demands? As we read Jesus' Sermon on the Mount in its blunt hardness, we are frightened: Can we really be Christians, Christ's disciples? We shall not look here for an easy answer—instead we shall, first, examine certain answers which we will find inadequate; second, attempt to find an answer in principle in Jesus' message as a whole; and third, face the difficult task of finding concrete guidance for our modern existence as Christians.

INADEQUATE ANSWERS

Christian exegetes will always profit by giving close attention to the opinions of Jewish scholars, since these have a natural affinity for Hebrew thought. Jesus appeared in his time as a Jew

ered "tolerable" or "bearable" in an age of scientific thinking. The "transcendent" God, rightly understood, is not only compatible with the "immanent" God who is present in the "depths of our existence," he is indeed necessary to bear up and fulfill our human existence. The same holds in the sphere of morals; the "heteronomous" will of God above us does not rule out our moral autonomy, but on the contrary first endows us with true freedom (cf. my essay "Christian Freedom in Paul" in the sequel to the present volume).

learned in Scripture; he engaged in disputations with scripture scholars, and drew on the Old Testament for his proofs. His manner, to be sure, was new and exciting. "He taught them as one who has authority, and not as the scribes" (Mk 1:22). How do modern Jewish scholars feel about the Sermon on the Mount? Through all their writings we encounter the opinion that Jesus' demands may be the expression of high moral and religious aspirations, but that they are unrealistic, and not life-enhancing. The Torah, the Jewish Law, is intended to establish God's will in Israel and among nations, and to penetrate and shape the world; but Jesus' excessive strictness makes any such thing impossible. Thus, J. Klausner, in his book on Jesus, writes: "Judaism also knows the ideal of love for the enemy . . . but Judaism never emphasized it to such a degree that it ultimately became too high an ideal for ordinary mankind, and even too high for the man of more than average moral calibre. The same applies to the ideal of 'stretching the other cheek.' Judaism also praised them 'who when affronted affront not again,' but it never emphasized the idea unduly, for it would be difficult for human society to exist with such a basic principle. Judaism did not forbid swearing and litigation, but enjoined 'a righteous yea or nay' and, in the person of Hillel, laid down the principle, 'Judge not thy neighbor till thou art come into his place.' Everything which Jesus ever uttered of this nature is Jewish ethical teaching, too; but his *over-*

emphasis was *not* Judaism, and, in fact, brought *non*-Judaism. When these extreme ethical standards are . . . taught as religious rules, while, at the same time, everyday life is conducted along completely different lines . . . it is inevitable that such ethical standards can make their appeal only to priests and recluses and the more spiritually minded among *individuals,* whose only interest is religion; while the rest of mankind all pursue a manner of life that is wholly secular or even pagan."[2]

Professor Schoeps, on the other hand, is of the opinion that the Sermon on the Mount does not intend to give commandments applicable in this world, but to describe the conditions that will prevail in the perfect world to come. "In keeping with the expectations of the Jews of his time, Jesus believed that the great turning point was imminent, and since he had mysterious knowledge of himself as the Son of man and the expected messiah, he had the right and duty to describe the nature of the great turning point in the beatitudes and antitheses. The Sermon on the Mount has no connection with any ethical problematic; it does not even yield positive aspects from which its relation to the Jewish law might be judged. But indirectly, one thing emerges nonetheless: when the kingdom comes, the Jewish law will 'cease'—to be broken. It will be capable of being fulfilled even in its most radical

[2] J. Klausner, *Jesus of Nazareth* (London, 1947), 392 f.

sense, because then duty and ability, Law and action, God's will and man's desire will coincide."[3] Unfortunately, this generous interpretation is untenable; for quite obviously Jesus' sayings and demands presuppose the conditions of this world. In the world to come there will be no litigation, no marriages, no enmities. Even so, this interpretation by a Jewish scholar shows him to consider it an impossibility that Jesus' demands could be met in *this* world. We must add in all fairness: most men today are likely to agree with him.

Not a few Protestant exegetes have attempted to turn this failure to advantage. They admit that Jesus' demands in the Sermon on the Mount are indeed impossible to meet; but they interpret this situation to mean: Jesus wanted to prepare men for the realization that they could not attain salvation by their own power, by way of obedience to the Law, but only through delivery by way of grace. Man, they say, is and remains a sinner, but he is saved by the blood of Jesus. This interpretation of the Sermon on the Mount has today generally been abandoned; H. Windisch disposed of it in his book *"The Meaning of the Sermon on the Mount."*[4] For this scholar eloquently

[3] H. J. Schoeps, "Jesus und das jüdische Gesetz," in *Aus frühchristlicher Zeit* (Tübingen, 1950), 212–220, this passage on p. 214.

[4] H. Windisch, *The Meaning of the Sermon on the Mount* (Philadelphia, 1951); further literature on the Sermon on the Mount is noted in R. Schnacken-

reminds the exegetes of their obligation to interpret the Sermon on the Mount not in terms of Paul, but in terms of its own content. Neither Matthew (Chapters 5–7) nor Luke (6:20–49) contain anything to the effect that man is incapable of obeying the law. Anyone who reads the "Sermon at the Mountain"[5] without preconceived notions will have to admit that Jesus did indeed intend that his demands ought to be met.

Nor do we any longer accept that liberal interpretation which claims that the only thing of importance is man's inner disposition, and that the Sermon on the Mount, although applicable in its own time, could not be reconciled to present civilization. "Over all the details there hovers an altogether unique purity, inwardness, and sensitivity, what in the most profound sense is

burg, *The Moral Teaching of the New Testament* (New York, 1965). See the important scholarly work of W. D. Davies, *The Setting of the Sermon on the Mount* (Cambridge, 1964); also, on New Testament ethics in general, C. Spicq, *Théologie morale du Nouveau Testament*, 2 vols. (Paris, 1965).

[5] This is what H. Schürmann calls Luke's version (because of its introduction, Lk 6:17, it is at times called "field address") in his essay "Warnung des Lukas vor der Falschlehre in der 'Predigt am Berg' in Lk 6:20–49," *Biblische Zeitschrift* 10 (1966), 57–81. We are in fact dealing with two versions of the same speech; cf. J. Dupont, *Les Béatitudes. Le problème littéraire—Les deux versions du Sermon sur la montagne et des Béatitudes* (Bruges-Louvain, 1958).

called ethos. There is no other literary expression of the same rounded character, the same energy of self-statement. Without any extreme intellectualism, the Sermon on the Mount represents a sensitivity and profundity in its symbolic language and unifying vision of nature and the world of the spirit, such as grows only out of the most accomplished humanity, such as only a mind can offer that is self-assured, that enters fully into all experience, and that draws all things into itself."[6] When we read such sentences as these which were written in 1921, we realize how far our notions of life are removed from such humanitarian thinking, and also—despite all those superlatives—how weak and inadequate is this judgment of Jesus. Was he indeed no more than a man of great inner fire, with an unsurpassable sensitivity for pure morality and inward piety?

Rudolf Bultmann's book *Jesus and the Word,* first published in 1926, served to clear the air. Bultmann speaks of the radical obedience which Jesus demands, an obedience that compels every man here and now to make his existential decision. Bultmann explicitly rejects the interpretation we mentioned earlier: "We cannot escape by saying, it depends only on the intention—thus separating the intention from the deed and seeing behind the deed an ideal of conduct which perhaps will be realized sometime in the future,

[6] O. Baumgarten, *Bergpredigt und Kultur der Gegenwart* (Tübingen, 1921), 117.

if only the good intention is kept alive in the man and he is more and more educated to that end . . . (Jesus) sees the concrete man in the crisis of decision, and the decision is not relative but absolute. . . . The requirements of the Sermon on the Mount do not present an ethical idealism, but bring to light the absolute character of the demands of God."[7] These statements of Bultmann do not reduce the full force of Jesus' demands—they place them before us without compromise. As we follow Bultmann's thought further, however, we come to discern a modern existential theology, which may well appeal to modern man and move him, but which does hardly reflect Jesus' own ideas. Jesus had no intention to propose to man demands with a specific content; he wanted only to confront man with God's radical claim, and so open man's eyes to the demands made on him in the given situation: "What God's will is, is not stated by an external authority, so that the content of the command is a matter of indifference, but man is trusted and expected to see for himself what God commands. God's requirements are intrinsically intelligible. And here the idea of obedience is first radically conceived."[8] God's demands "arise quite simply from the crisis of decision in which man stands before God. This answer has meaning, of course, only for him who sees man, who sees himself, forced to this neces-

[7] R. Bultmann, *Jesus and the Word* (New York, 1934).
[8] *Ibid.*

136

sity of decision. Its meaning is simply that this moment of decision contains all that is necessary for the decision, since in it the whole of life is at stake."[9] No, Jesus lays claim to the authoritative interpretation of the divine will ("But *I* say to you . . ."), and explicates that will with comments on several commandments (Mt 5:21–48).[10] It is true, of course, that the personal summons confronts each individual with the special decisions that must be made in his own circumstances, and only these circumstances give to God's will its full radical character. To judge by the testimony of the Apostolic Fathers, as early as the second century,[11] it has always been the view of the

[9] *Ibid.*

[10] Some scholars hold the view that the words "But I say to you . . ." is merely a formula of rabbinical discussion; thus M. Smith, *Tannaitic Parallels to the Gospels* (Philadelphia, 1951); more balanced and aware of the distinctions, D. Daube, *The New Testament and Rabbinic Judaism* (London, 1956), 55–62; see also W. D. Davies, *loc. cit.,* 102 f. Also V. E. Hasler, "Das Herzstück der Bergpredigt, Mt 5, 21–48," *Theologische Zeitschrift* 15 (1959), 90–106.

[11] Thus, in the old "Teaching of the Lord through the Twelve Apostles" (The Didache, probably toward the end of the first century), the "way of life" begins with the double commandment of love, followed by the "Golden Rule," after which these directives are explicated with passages from the Sermon on the Mount (Chapter 1). Passages from the Old Testament are used to drive home the exhortations of the

Church that Jesus' demands exceed the Law of the Old Testament in content as well, and that they are binding in their concrete content.

There has never been a lack of attempts to interpret Jesus' demands literally and so to put them into practice. In particular the commandment to love your enemy and to forego retaliation (Mt 5:38–48; Lk 6:27–30) has again and again given man food for serious thought, and has inspired social reforms and movements for peace among nations. In modern times, we may recall the social program of Count Leo Tolstoi,[12] and the radical pacificism of many Christian groups including even the refusal to render military service. But did Jesus indeed intend with his moral demands to change earthly conditions, legal

"way of life and death," as follows: "Do not transgress the commandments of the Lord, preserve what you have received, do not add to it nor take away from it!" (4:12). At the end the point is repeated: "Your prayers, your almsgiving and all your actions you shall perform as you are told in the gospel of our Lord" (15:4). Cf. further V. E. Hasler, *Gesetz und Evangelium in der alten Kirche bis Origines* (Zurich, 1953); P. G. Verweijs, *Evangelium und neues Gesetz in der ältesten Christenheit bis auf Marcion* (Utrecht, 1960).

[12] Cf. H. Weinel, *Jesus in the 19th Century and After* (Edinburgh, 1914); J. Ackermann, *Tolstoj und das Neue Testament* (Leipzig, 1927); K. Hamburger, *Leo Tolstoj, Gestalt und Problem* (Munich, 1950).

order, social structure,[13] international relations, or the constitution of the world in general? If we interpret the Sermon on the Mount in a "worldly" fashion, we arrive at the threshold of a Utopia. But everything else we know of Jesus' teachings and conduct shows that he was a realist, who did not wish to interfere—at least not directly—in the affairs of the world, a world which even then was far from ideal.[14] His radicalism is concerned with man himself, man who is to gain a new understanding of himself before God and among his fellows. Jesus wants to make man radical in his moral aspiration; but as every man lives in his own time, in his own environment, the radical demands made in the Sermon on the Mount raise this problem: What did Jesus mean, what did he intend with them?

Our short survey of recent views has made us aware how difficult and important it is to decide whether Jesus' demands can in effect be met. It may be that the Catholic Church has not always escaped the temptation to weaken Jesus' radical demands in a cheap manner. It is hardly possible to claim that Jesus' moral teachings are funda-

[13] Cf. the "socialist" interpretation of Jesus in K. Kautsky, M. Maurenbrecher, L. Ragaz and others; see H. Weinel, *loc. cit.;* J. Leipoldt, *Vom Jesusbild der Gegenwart* (Leipzig, 1925), 60–122. On the Sermon on the Mount, see L. Ragaz, *Die Bergpredigt* (Bern, 1945).

[14] Cf. R. Schnackenburg, *The Moral Teaching of the New Testament.*

mentally no more than an interpretation of the
Natural Law, giving it concreteness in Christian
terms. The distance between a natural ethics and
Christian morality is much larger than that. An
ethics that starts out from the nature of man
will never be able to provide grounds for those demands of Jesus in the Sermon on the Mount which
attack, challenge, even shock the natural man.[15]

The interpretation of individual sentences and
statements in the Sermon on the Mount depends
largely on the interpretation of the Sermon as a
whole; it was a decisive statement of Jesus, and
probably has been put together quite early in the
work of the early Church; besides, it was given
a special formulation by Luke and even more so
by Matthew.[16] We cannot here trace this tradi-

---

[15] Cf. R. Schnackenburg, "Die neutestamentlich Sitten-
lehre in ihrer Eigenart im Vergleich zu einer natür-
lichen Ethik," in *Moraltheologie und Bibel,* ed. J.
Stelzenberger (Paderborn, 1964), 39–69.

[16] Cf. the work by J. Dupont cited in note 5, above. On
Luke, see H. Kahlefeld, *Der Jünger. Eine Auslegung
der Rede Lk 6, 20–49* (Frankfurt, 1962); H. Schür-
mann, *loc. cit.,* note 5; on Matthew, see J. Kürzinger,
"Zur Komposition der Bergpredigt nach Matthäus,"
in *Biblica* 40 (1959), 569–589; G. Barth, "Das Gesetz-
verständnis des Evangelisten Matthäus," in *Über-
lieferung und Auslegung im Matthäusevangelium*
(Neukirchen, 1960), 54–154; W. Trilling, *Das wahre
Israel* (Munich, 1964), 165–211; G. Strecker, *Der
Weg der Gerechtigkeit* (Göttingen, 1962), 130–166;
W. D. Davies, *loc. cit.,* note 4.

tion, and the factors and tendencies that went into it; nor can we follow at greater length the divergent views of Luke and Matthew; here we are concerned with Jesus' own intention. We must, then, place the Sermon on the Mount into the total framework of Jesus' message and proclamation.

THE SERMON ON THE MOUNT IN THE FRAMEWORK OF JESUS' MESSAGE

Jesus brought a religious message which Mark has strikingly summarized in his account of the beginning of Jesus' public ministry: "The time is fulfilled, and the kingdom of God is at hand; repent, and believe in the gospel" (Mk 1:15). Jesus says, then, that with his appearance the time of the final days has been accomplished as the prophets promised, and that God's kingdom, his blessed dominion, is near. Jesus' own work marks this time of final salvation. Other passages also allow the same conclusion, that Jesus regarded his own appearance as the fulfillment of the prophetic promises, especially those of Isaiah.[17] Jesus is the bearer of joy of whom we read in Isaiah 52:7:

"How beautiful upon the mountains
    are the feet of him who brings good tidings

[17] Cf. Mt 11:4 ff.; Lk 4:18–21; 10:23 f. See R. Schnackenburg, *God's Rule and Kingdom* (New York, 1963); N. Brox, "Das messianische Selbstverständnis des

141

who publishes peace, who brings good tidings of good,
  who publishes salvation,
who says to Zion, 'Your God reigns.'"

Those various expressions—peace, bliss, salvation—
all signify the same thing: the definitive salvation which God gives to man by taking possession
of his kingdom.

The peculiarity of Jesus' eschatological proclamation lies in this, that salvation is beginning to
become a reality through his own coming, in his
person and in his work, though its consummation
still remains in the future. God's dominion reveals
itself in signs: the forgiveness of sins, the healing
of the sick, and the casting out of demons. Jesus
once says: "If it is by the finger of God that I cast
out demons, then the kingdom of God has come
upon you" (Lk 11:20). But the perfect dominion
of God, the cosmic realm, still remains in the
future. Jesus promises it as the great and imminent event; then God's glory will be revealed over
the whole world, and full salvation will be bestowed on those who are receptive. In this way,
Jesus' message becomes God's final offer of salvation to mankind: Repent and believe in the gospel!

This proclamation of God's kingdom thus also

historischen Jesus," in *Vom Messias zum Christus*
(Vienna, 1964), 165–201; G. E. Ladd, *Jesus and the
Kingdom* (New York, 1964); A. Vögtle, "Exegetische
Erwägungen über das Wissen und Selbstbewusstsein
Jesu," in *Gott in Welt* I (*Festgabe für K. Rahner*)
(Freiburg i.Br., 1964), 608–667.

contains the source of Jesus' moral imperative. Since God grants forgiveness now, and signs of salvation occur now, therefore salvation is already effective, not just an empty promise for the future. The "acceptable year of the Lord" (Lk 4:19) begins with Jesus. But since God does not yet grant full salvation, salvation remains *an offer,* that is, a promise after all, the promise of full salvation and the renewal of the world (Mt 19:28). Only he who does God's will now, in the hour of salvation, shall enter into God's kingdom (Mt 11:21).[18]

The Sermon on the Mount, too, is included in the totality of Jesus' message. The Beatitudes at its beginning (Mt 5:3-10) are nothing else than the promise of full salvation, the consummation of God's kingship, for those who are ready and receptive. "Blessed are the poor in spirit, for theirs is the kingdom of heaven. . . ." The blessings of God's kingdom are described in image after image. "They shall be comforted, they shall inherit the earth, they shall be satisfied, obtain mercy, see God, be called sons of God." And again, finally, "blessed are those who are perse-

---

[18] Cf. H. Windisch, "Die Sprüche vom Eingehen in das Reich Gottes," *Zeitschrift für die neutestamentliche Wissenschaft* 27 (1928), 163–192. Matthew 7:21 is his own formulation, as we can see by comparing it with Lk 6:46, more radical, combined with the eschatological saying "Lord, Lord" (7:22; see also 25:11), and conformed to it. The idea of "fulfilling God's will" is typical of Matthew, also cf. W. Trilling, *loc. cit.,* note 16, 187–192.

cuted for righteousness' sake, for theirs is the kingdom of heaven." But to share in these promises, men must meet certain conditions. Matthew himself interprets the Beatitudes as a moral summons to the listeners.[19]

The point becomes even clearer in the sayings dealing with man's entry into God's kingdom. Jesus makes high and heavy demands of the aspirants, using the image of the entry into God's kingdom. "Unless your righteousness exceeds that of the scribes and Pharisees, you will never enter the kingdom of heaven" (5:20). "Enter by the narrow gate" (7:13); and still more pointedly in Luke 13:24: "Strive to enter by the narrow door; for many, I tell you, will seek to enter and will not

[19] Originally, the beatitudes were neither a guide of good conduct for their audience (Mt) nor a "social" manifesto for the poor and oppressed (Lk), but the explication of Jesus' religious message of salvation, the "evangel" as such. Each of the two evangelists gave them a special complexion, aimed at his readers. Cf. J. Dupont, *Les Béatitudes*, 322 f; "The two orientations take their starting point and justification from a basic text, the sense of which does not fully coincide with either interpretation. . . . The '*Woes*' are in harmony with the special interpretation of the beatitudes in Luke's version, while the additions whereby Matthew raises the meaning of the beatitudes to a moral level, are in harmony with his interpretation of the evangel." Dupont calls the original meaning of the beatitudes "messianic."

144

be able."[20] And again in Matthew's Sermon on the Mount: "Not every one who says to me, 'Lord, Lord,' shall enter the kingdom of heaven, but he who does the will of my Father who is in heaven" (7:12). The Sermon on the Mount is a mighty appeal to all who would enter God's kingdom that they should bend all their efforts to seek God's kingdom. "Seek first his kingdom and his righteousness, and all these things shall be yours as well" (6:33). We now understand better why Jesus hardly mentions conditions on earth. Untroubled by his own one-sidedness, he proclaims God's holy and absolute will, and summons mankind to the most important, the most urgent task that they are to meet at this present hour.

Yes, at this present hour! Only, we must not compute the hour by our human calendar. The hour of salvation is the presence of Jesus. The urgency of the statement in his sermon, that the

[20] Luke reports these words with reference to someone's question whether many will be saved (v. 23), and thus corrects that mistaken view: man should not raise questions but bend all his efforts to belong among the saved. Matthew introduces the Jewish doctrine of two gates: "For the gate is wide and the way is easy, that leads to destruction, and those who enter by it are many. For the gate is narrow and the way is hard, that leads to life, and those who find it are few" (Mt 7:13). Again each of the two evangelists has in his own way brought Jesus stirring words home to his readers.

145

kingdom of God is *near*, has led some interpreters to the conclusion that he expected the end of the world in the immediate future. This is the thesis of eschatologism; according to that thesis, Jesus made a mistake concerning the time of the world's end. Other texts, however, contradict this view, since they leave the time of the end indefinite and reserved to the wisdom of the Father (Mk 13:32; Lk 17:20 f.). The impression of the end being expected immediately stems from the prophetic manner of the sermon, which attempts to impress upon the listeners the future that is coming. This manner of speaking is intended to make them certain of God's unfailing promise, and aware of his irrefutable claim, regardless of when the "end" is to come.[21] We have to free ourselves of our own ideas of time, and learn to think in God's categories as the Bible does. Salvation has come definitively ("eschatologically") with Jesus, and thus final salvation is approaching us with certainty and irresistibly. The parables of growth (Mk 4:26–32) illustrate the point: as surely as the sowing of the seed is followed by the harvest, by its own inner dynamic

---

[21] H. Schürmann therefore is correct in speaking of a "standing expectation" which counts upon the end at every moment; he sees it as more basic than all "imminent expectation": *Das Gebet des Herrn* (Freiburg, n.d.) 125 f. in note 140. See also E. Neuhäusler, *Anspruch und Antwort Gottes* (Düsseldorf, 1962), 37–42; R. Schnackenburg, "Naherwartung," *LThK* VII (1962), 777–779.

and consistency, just as surely God's kingdom will come, by God's will and power which become visible even in Jesus' works.[22]

New Testament ethics assumes its true character only when seen from this "eschatological" point of view. It is not a stop-gap ethic, not an emergency morality to apply during the short interval before the end when all earthly matters become totally irrelevant. But it is an "eschatological" ethic, in which all earthly matters reveal their inconclusive, inconstant, and invalid nature. "The form of this world is passing away," says Paul (1 Cor 7:31). In this earthly situation, in this terrestrial-historical condition that marks our human existence, there must be no final bond to earthly goods. God alone is the absolute purpose of our being. "No one can serve two masters. . . . You cannot serve God and mammon," says Jesus (Mt 6:24). Therefore, the first and greatest commandment is to love God, with all one's heart, all one's soul, all one's mind. Now, at this moment when God establishes his kingdom, God's will is to be done by Jesus' disciples, purely and completely.

Thus there appears a radical or, if you will, rigorous trait in Jesus' language. Yet Jesus does not present himself to men simply as a new law-

---

[22] Cf. N. A. Dahl, "The Parables of Growth," *Studia Theologica* 5 (1951), 132–166; R. Schnackenburg, *God's Rule and Kingdom* (New York, 1963); E. Jüngel, *Paulus und Jesus* (Tübingen, 1964), 139–154.

giver, but also and primarily as the bearer of God's salvation. It is only because he offers to mankind God's love and salvation that he is able and resolved to make high demands on them in God's name. How else could he claim that his yoke is easy and his burden light (Mt 11:30), even while making almost superhuman demands? This tension appears in the structure of Jesus' sermons: he proclaims to men the infinite mercy of God (Lk 15), and calls on them for generous and grateful love in return. He devotes himself even to the despised tax collectors and prostitutes (Mk 2:16; Lk 7:36–50; Mt 21:31), but he expects in return that they will sin no more. In the time of the eschaton, God asks for much because he gives much—he demands great things because he grants and promises still greater things.

We must consider one other matter. To many of those who heard the Sermon on the Mount, Jesus' call for undivided service to God meant at the same time the call to join Jesus' disciples and to follow him.[23] These men then learned in concrete terms what God's demand meant for them personally. In this respect, the Sermon on the Mount is a general program whose specific details must be filled in for each individual. The Sermon is a manifesto addressed to all men, but must be adapted to the historical situation. Many of the statements in the Sermon on the Mount appear in a new light simply by virtue of Jesus' own con-

[23] Cf. the preceding chapter "The Imitation of Christ."

duct. Turning the other cheek (Mt 5:39) does not mean that we must approve injustice (cf. Jn 18:22 f.). The prohibition to be angry (Mt 5:22) still leaves room for a "holy anger" (cf. Mk 3:5). Jesus' fiery polemics against the godless leaders of the people show that man must stand up for God's rights with courage and persistence. Even the Church fathers recognized the important principle that Jesus explained his words by his actions.

This brings us to the language of his Sermon on the Mount. Without diminishing in the least the tremendous impact of his words it must be stated that Jesus, in keeping with the methods of instruction of his day, employed images and examples that must not be taken literally. He gives three images for the idea to forego retaliation: "If any one strikes you on the right cheek, turn to him the other also; and if any one should sue you and take your coat, let him have your cloak as well; and if any one forces you to go one mile, go with him two miles" (Mt 5:39 ff.). Jesus uses hyperbole to make his exhortations clear; but the images remain images, and we understand readily that his image of the law suit does not mean Jesus wanted to do away with all jurisdiction. Or are we to believe that Jesus would allow prayer only in the secluded chamber, forbid public almsgiving altogether, or recommend to those who fast the use of ointments (cf. Mt 6:18–18)? This imagery does of course raise various problems of interpretation. The exchange about divorce which is specifically reported by both Mark and Matthew (Mk 10:1–12; Mt 19:1–9) makes clear that Jesus prohibited divorce on principle, departing thereby from current Jewish practice. Is the same thing true for the prohibition of swearing, which is reported only in the Sermon on the Mount (Mt 5:33–37)? Or did he want only to do away with the private abuse of swearing which was then rampant among Jews? When we are faced with such problems which exegesis cannot solve with certainty, we will have to be guided by the interpretation of the Church. In explaining Jesus' imagery, we must not destroy Jesus' radical intention, but neither may we absolutize the images. We must try to grasp Jesus' spirit as it expresses itself in this language, and must apply his instructions to our own historical and personal situation without breaking faith with his intention.

This brings us to the last part of our reflections: How are we to apply the demands of the Sermon on the Mount to our own Christian existence today without weakening them, but also without doing them violence and ourselves becoming religious fanatics?

THE SERMON ON THE MOUNT
AS A GUIDE TODAY

The evangelists themselves show us how to apply the words of Jesus to a new audience. Matthew adapted the Sermon on the Mount to his Judeo-Christian readers, Luke to his pagan-

Christian public. The third evangelist omitted several matters that were incomprehensible and unfit for the pagan audiences of that day, yet he did not misrepresent Jesus' spirit.[24] Quite the contrary—he has brought out with unmatched power the one most needful thing: the commandment of love. After the blessings and the warnings, he turns at once to the law of love and uses the most extreme instance, the love of one's enemies, to show how far our love for our fellow man must go in imitation of God's unfathomable and paradoxical love for us. He gives a new formulation to the statements reported also by Matthew, a formulation which sounds contemporary still today: "But love your enemies, and do good, and lend, expecting nothing in return; and your reward will be great, and you will be sons of the Most High; for he is kind to the ungrateful and the selfish" (Lk 6:35). Love of enemy obviously concerns unlovely people who yet need our help; through them, God calls us. How we help them—by a personal act, or by giving material aid—depends entirely on the circumstances; what matters is that we hear God's call in its uncompromising nature, and act by his example. At root, the love of one's enemies expresses only a certain aspect of the love of neighbor. The classic exam-

[24] See the book by Kahlefeld cited in note 16, above; also H. W. Bartsch, "Feldrede und Bergpredigt. Redaktionsarbeit in Luke 6," *Theologische Zeitschrift* 16 (1960), 5–18.

ple is the parable of the good Samaritan; the beaten Jew by the wayside is his benefactor's enemy, an enemy even of his nation—for there was then hatred between the Jews and the Samaritans. The love that Jesus asks from us after God's example always conceals a tiny seed of selfless, self-conquering love. In this sense we must ultimately understand also the double commandment to love God and neighbor. The words "Love thy neighbor as thyself!" do not intend to set a limit to our love of neighbor, but to give it the greatest possible motivation: everything you would do for yourself you ought to do for your neighbor as well! With that, all questions become unnecessary—everyone knows at once what is demanded of him.[25]

[25] R. Bultmann, in his *Jesus and the Word,* quotes the beautiful words of S. Kierkegaard: "When we are commanded to love our neighbor *like ourselves,* the commandment springs open the lock of self-love as if with a passkey, and robs man of self-love. If the commandment of love of neighbor were expressed any other way than with the words *as thyself*— which are so easily pronounced and yet contain the tension of eternity—the commandment could not overcome self-love. There is no escaping this *as thyself;* with the judgment edge of eternity it penetrates into the innermost nook where a man loves himself; it leaves no excuses to self-love, no door of escape. . . . This *as thyself*—no wrestler can lay hold on his opponent as firmly, inescapably as this commandment lays hold on self-love."

We thus have found an important, even decisive principle for the application of Jesus' demands: *All the demands of the Sermon on the Mount are in turn summed up in the greatest commandment—to love.* To have given this commandment the double thrust, of love of God and love of neighbor equally important, is in this indissoluble union a new thing, a creative act of Jesus.[26] It gives us an immediate guide for our conduct. True love of God shows itself in love of neighbor, even to the point of loving one's enemies; and our love of neighbor in turn gives us the assurance that we love the invisible God. If we think through these thoughts of Jesus about love, the demands of the Sermon on the Mount will become transparently clear to us, simple and yet new in each new situation. He who truly loves God knows what God wants him to do here and now. In this lies the truth of Augustine's words, "Love and do what you will!" They are bold words and can easily be misused; but to those who love truly they are a golden key.

As we survey the vast field of morality, and think of the complex situations we meet in life,

[26] None of the parallels adduced from Judaism approach Jesus' decision. Lk 10:27, where the scribe of his own accord cites the double commandment, can hardly be advanced, since this pericope is probably nothing else than a different version of Mk 12:28–31, adapted to the context by Luke or his model. Cf. R. Schnackenburg, *The Moral Teaching of the New Testament.*

many specific questions must of course be left open. But we might give thought to certain special stresses in Jesus' moral teaching, matters which obviously were particularly close to his heart, and which also show how close he was to life and how well he knew man. Jesus recognized that wealth was one of man's most dangerous temptations. We may recall once again the word of the two masters: "You cannot serve God and mammon." Near it, Matthew has placed another word, about treasures: "Lay up for yourselves treasures in heaven. . . . For where your treasure is, there will your heart be also" (Mt 6:19–21). Every Christian must examine himself and ask again and again: How am I using my earthly goods? What does God want me to do? The leveling effect of a morality grown bourgeois can be seen in the meaning of the word "alms," which in common usage means a small pittance, but in the gospel may at times mean the surrender of one's entire fortune to the poor (Lk 12:33). The words, "It is easier for a camel to go through the eye of a needle than for a rich man to enter the kingdom of God" (Mk 10:25), is an intentional paradox and hyperbole based on Jesus' own experience: Jesus considers wealth to be extremely dangerous to any man.

Jesus also takes a pessimistic view of the desire to appear great before men. In the Sermon on the Mount, he castigates the showy piety of certain groups of Pharisees who keep to all observances only "in order to be seen" (Mt 6:1). Such a disposition makes a complete surrender to God impossible, and leads to that hypocrisy which Jesus attacks repeatedly. He warns his own disciples not to strive for power. "You know that those who are supposed to rule over the Gentiles lord it over them, and their great men exercise authority over them. But it shall not be so among you; but whoever would be great among you must be your servant, and whoever would be first among you must be slave of all" (Mk 10:42 ff.). Again, these words must be interpreted in Jesus' spirit: he did not intend to condemn all leaders. He rejected neither Nicodemus the ruler of the Jews nor the wealthy Joseph of Arimathea; but he condemned lust for power in the strongest terms and branded it as incompatible with the discipleship to which he was calling man. The early Church, too, had its leaders; and to this day we can sense how they took constant warning from those words of Jesus. In Luke's gospel, the quarrel among the disciples over their rank, and Jesus' answer to them, are shifted to the evening of the Last Supper—a hint to the heads of the Christian communities to practice the duty of brotherly service even during the community assembly for the holy meal.[27] In this manner, the Gospels themselves applied the words and teachings of Jesus to the situation of the early Church, and interpreted them in the light of the Church's

[27] Cf. H. Schürmann, *Der Abendmahlsbericht Lukas 22, 7–38* (Leipzig, 1955), 60–75.

life. Our task is the same: each of us must give thought to his own situation and personal obligations, and must ever anew submit to the impact and the judgment of the words which the Lord spoke in the Sermon on the Mount.

Let us finally take a look at Jesus' attitude toward sex. It might almost be thought surprising that he does not warn more often and more strongly against the destructive power of this in itself God-given drive. The irresistible power of the drive was as strong then as it is now; but Jesus did not see it as the chief enemy of man's salvation. More than once he encountered genuine repentance, an honest turning back among those who had stumbled—which he recognized as a better toehold for God's grace than hardened pride and a heart in which love has died. But he would not tolerate any challenge of the divine ordinance which is the guarantee of human happiness and peace. He condemned unbridled desire as much as the actual sin, and his attitude concerning divorce was unyielding (Mt 5:27–32).[28]

[28] Cf. J. Dupont, *Mariage et Divorce dans l'Évangile* (Bruges, 1959); M. Zerwick, "De matrimonio et divortio in Evangelio," *Verbum Domini* 38 (1960), 193–212. The so-called "immorality clause" in Mt 5:32, 19:9, whatever difficulties its explanation may present, is not an exception to the prohibition of divorce. J. Bonsirven, in his *Le divorce dans le Nouveau Testament* (Paris, 1948), first suggested a solution since then widely adopted (it concerns so-called forbidden, legally invalid marriages); it has

This last point reminds us once again of the question whether Jesus' demands can be met by man. There remains a tension between the promise of salvation and the moral imperative. As human beings, we are exposed to temptations even under the new dispensation, under the salvific rule of Christ, and we feel how weak we are. We will be tempted to say: Jesus' demands cannot be met—and this is a form of temptation! At such a time we shall do well to recall the words: "With men it is impossible, but not with God" (Mk 10:27). Together with his demands, Jesus gives us also God's power—or, in post-Pentecostal terms, the Holy Spirit—by which we become capable of obeying the law of Christ. And finally: God's mercy does not stop before Christ's weak disciple. Therefore, we must take nothing from the holiness and hardness of Christ's demands, and must face them in our own position and actual situation. But we should also know that we are in the keeping of God's love, who wants only our salvation, and who will love us until the day of our full deliverance.

been developed further by H. Baltensweiler, "Die Ehebruchsklausel bei Matthäus," *Theologische Zeitschrift* 15 (1959), 34–356; see, most recently, J. B. Bauer, "De coniugali foedere quid edixerit Matthaeus?" *Verbum Domini* 44 (1966), 74–78.

VI

Christian Perfection According to Matthew

Perfection is often called the highest goal of Christian endeavor, "the highest religious and moral achievement attainable for the individual man on this earth."[1] It is often mentioned in connection with the evangelic counsels—voluntary poverty, virginity, and perfect obedience. If these counsels are adopted as a permanent form of life, by a solemn vow, we speak of a "state of perfection"; and this has given rise to many misunderstandings. Moral theology has long since established that the "counsels of perfection" with the orders are by no means perfection itself, but only ways and means to attain perfection. The expression "state of perfection" does not mean "that all those who have taken this road are thereby more perfect, or will become more perfect—and even less that they are better merely

---

[1] F. Tillman, *Die Idee der Nachfolge Christi* (Düsseldorf, 1949), 193; see the entire section on perfection, 190–197.

for taking this road—than are those who remain in the world.''[2] Each man, in this view, can and ought to become perfect in his walk of life, and this goal would be more readily within his reach in proportion as he performed the duties of his walk of life with loyalty and devotion. The essence of Christian perfection, further, is love of God and neighbor.[3]

Christian perfection so understood does certainly correspond to the spirit of the New Testament, and thus may express the Christian endeavor. But the question remains whether we are not here choosing a concept that plays no part in Jesus' message, but rather derives from Greek ethical doctrine. Since this kind of perfection can never be attained completely on earth, it seems to be an ideal that is not attainable in practice; and modern man, realistic and factual as he is, may find such an ideal discouraging.

It is worth our while, therefore, to trace the Biblical concept of perfection. It has its roots in the Old Testament, and stems from Hebraic-Semitic thought. This thought follows other roads than

---

[2] *Ibid.*, 203; see the entire section on perfection and the counsels of perfection, 198–205.

[3] *Ibid.*, 194: "Thus the perfection of Christian life is primarily judged by love." He bases himself on Thomas Aquinas, Summa Theol. II–II, qu. 188, a. 1. This doctrine is in the best tradition of the Church. The professional ethics of the laity have, however, often been neglected; on this subject, see now A. Auer, *Christsein im Beruf* (Düsseldorf, 1966).

does Greek ethics; in many respect it is closer to today's "existential" thought than to the Greeks.[4] We encounter the word "perfect" only twice in the gospels. The first time is in the general summons in the Sermon on the Mount: "You, therefore, must be perfect, as your heavenly Father is perfect" (Mt 5:48); the other is in Jesus' answer to the rich young ruler: "If you would be perfect, go, sell what you possess . . ." (Mt 19:21). We are justified to see it as the expression of the evangelist's own special views; and since he betrays a strong interest in Jesus' moral teachings, we may also regard him as a competent early Christian interpreter of Jesus' message. But we must keep in mind that he comes from a background of Jewish thought, as we now try to determine what he understands by "perfect."

The Hebrew term for "perfect" (*tamim*) probably comes from the language of the sacrifice. In the cultic instructions of Leviticus, and elsewhere

[4] Cf. the first chapter of this book. Literature on the concept of perfection in the Bible: B. Rigaux, "Révélation des mystères et la perfection à Qumran et dans le Nouveau Testament," *New Testament Studies* 4 (1957/58), 237–262; P. J. du Plessis, *Teleios. The Idea of Perfection in the New Testament* (Kampen, 1959); K. Prümm, "Das neutestamentliche Sprach- und Begriffsproblem der Vollkommenheit," *Biblica* 44 (1963), 76–92; G. Delling in *ThWNT* VIII (Stuttgart, 1965), 68–80.

as well,[5] sacrificial animals without blemish are prescribed. This is precisely what the Hebrew means to convey: that something be untouched, complete, undiminished in its constitution and its value. While the Greek conceives of "perfection" as an ideal which reality can at best approach, the Hebrew by contrast starts out from reality which he considers in its original integrity. It is no longer perfect when it is in any way damaged or spoiled (cf. Jos 10:13; Ez 15:5). Here, too, the Hebrew idea of wholeness prevails: the individual things are parts of the whole, and if they drop out of the whole there is destruction of the order, and decay.[6] To a world of thought which takes this view of integrity, the striving for perfection means something else than it does to idealistic Greek thought: it means to hold on to, or regain, an originally given unity and reality, and not the gradual approximation of an ideal goal. This is the world of thought in which the first evangelist, too, has his roots; and for this reason we shall trace the Old Testament concept of perfection somewhat more fully.

[5] Ex 12:5; 29:1; Lv 1:3, 10; 3:1, 6, 9; 4:3, 23, 32, etc.; Nem 6:14; 19:2 etc.; Ex 43:22, 25; 45:18, 23; 46:4, 6, 13. Cf. W. Eichrodt, *Theology of the Old Testament* (Philadelphia, 1961–67); G. Delling *loc. cit.*, 73.

[6] Cf. T. Boman, *Hebrew Thought Compared with Greek* (Philadelphia, 1960).

THE OLD TESTAMENT FOUNDATION
OF THE CONCEPT OF PERFECTION

Let us examine more closely the concept *tamim* insofar as it applies to religious and moral concerns. To be "blameless" before the Lord (Deut 18:13) means to belong to him wholeheartedly, without practicing idolatry, sorcery, and other abominations (cf. 18:9–12). Such total surrender must be constant: "Fear the Lord, and serve him in sincerity and in faithfulness. . . ." (Jos 24:14). To give one's whole heart to God in its purity, unblemished by alien thoughts and inclinations: this is what the substantive *tom* expresses, and what we might translate with "innocence, simplicity." This is how the Lord speaks to Solomon: "If you will walk before me, as David your father walked, with integrity of heart (*b'tom-l'bab*) and uprightness (*b'-joscher*), doing according to all that I have commanded you . . . then I shall establish your royal throne over Israel forever . . ." (1 Kg 9:4 f.). Guileless and sincere talk, too, is described with this word.[7] Integrity (*tom*) and uprightness (*joscher*), according to Psalm 25:21, protect the faithful who is waiting for the Lord. The Old Testament term for just conduct, *saddik*, also implies this exclusive and total surrender of the *tamim* to God. Of Noah we read: "Noah was a righteous man, blameless in his generation; Noah walked with God" (Gen 6:9; cf. Sir 44:17).

---

[7] Cf. Gen 20:5 f.; 2 Sam 15:11; 3 Kgs 22:34; 2 Chron 18:33.

Exemplary conduct could be described in these terms: righteousness before God and a life united with God.

The passage quoted last shows that the Israelites considered such "perfect" conduct a human possibility. God exhorts Abraham: "Walk before me, and be blameless" (Gen 17:1); and the father of Israel did as he was told. Many rabbis interpret the passage to mean that there was nothing objectionable about Abraham, except his foreskin, and when he had been circumcised he was called "perfect."[8] David, too, can say of himself: "I was blameless before him" (2 Sam 22:24); "For I have kept the ways of the Lord, and have not wickedly departed from my God. For all his ordinances were before me, and from his statutes I did not turn aside." What is decisive, then, is always God's will and judgment; man must live up to the image that God has of him. "To walk blamelessly" and "to do what is right" is the same thing (Ps 15:2; cf. Prov 2:21). Job calls himself a just and blameless man (Job 12:4). In the same way the substantives "blamelessness" and "righteousness" occupy parallel positions.

The more the Torah, the Jewish Law, becomes the expression of God's will and the standard of conduct, the more is "blamelessness" identified with irreproachable obedience to the law. To be

[8] See sources cited in P. Billerbeck, *Kommentar zum Neuen Testament aus Talmud und Midrasch* I (Munich, 1922), 386.

blameless is the same as to keep the law of the Lord (Ps 119:1). "Walking" and "way" are the most usual Old Testament images for human conduct, and we encounter such expressions as "those of blameless ways" (Prov 11:20), "a righteous man walks in integrity" (Prov 20:7, cf. 28:18), and "the way that is blameless" (Ps 101:2, 6).[9] In the rabbinical tradition, a "perfect just man" is one who has kept the entire Torah; patriarchs especially were thought to belong in that category.[10]

The Qumran texts, too, speak frequently of "perfection" or "righteousness" and perfect or righteous men, and once again in connection with the images of "walking" and "way." Here too we find the expressions "ways of the righteous,"[11] "those who walk in blamelessness,"[12] or "in perfection (of the way)."[13] This distinctive vocabulary is in Qumran applied only to members of the community of God; the community has "a house of perfection and truth in Israel" (1 QS 8:9). The references in Dam 20:2, 5, 7 to the "perfect men of holiness" sound as if they meant the community itself (see also 7:4 f., "in holy perfection");[14] the

---

[9] Cf. F. Nötscher, *Gotteswege und Menschenwege in der Bibel und in Qumran* (Bonn, 1958), esp. 50–52.

[10] Rosh ha-shana 16b Bar. (Billerbeck I, 50 f.); Shabbath 55a and further references in Billerbeck I, 814 f.

[11] 1 QS 4:22; 1 QSa 1:28; 1 QM 14:7; 1 QH 1:36.

[12] 1 QS 1:8; 2:2; 3:9; 9:19; 1 QSb 1:2; 5:22.

[13] I QS 5:24; 8:21; 9:6, 8, 9.

[14] Cf. Ch. Rabin, *The Zadokite Documents* (Oxford, 1954), to Dam VII, 5 (26 f., note 2).

same holds for 1 QS 8:15.[15] Such walking in perfection is possible only if these elect know God's way, that is, have the right understanding of the law; but such true knowledge is revealed to them by God.[16]

Even more significant is the fact that the members of the Qumran community are convinced, despite their heroic efforts, that man is by himself incapable of walking in perfection; God has to justify him and to grant him grace. Accordingly, the final psalm of the community rule says: "As concerns me, my justification is in God's hands, and in his hands is the perfection of my ways" (1 QS 11:2); "from his hands comes the perfection of the way" (ibid., 10 f.); and there is a similar passage in the Hodajoth (songs of praise): "And I have understood that there is no justice with men, and no man walks in righteousness. All the works of justice are with the highest God, but the way of man is uncertain, except by the spirit which God created for him, to make the way of man righteous, so that men may know all his works in the strength of his power, and the fullness of his mercy upon all the sons in whom he is pleased" (1 QH 4:30–33).[17] Here the moral-

---

[15] P. Wernberg-Möller, *The Manual of Discipline* (Leiden, 1957) would amend the text to Dam XX, 2:7 (34; 42; 131, note 57). Cf. on style Nötscher, *loc. cit.*, 80.

[16] Cf. B. Rigaux, *loc. cit.*, note 4, above; P. J. du Plessis, *loc. cit.*, 104–115.

[17] Translated from E. Lohse, *Die Texte aus Qumran* (Darmstadt, 1964), 129.

ity of the Torah is made richer by a deeply religious thought which did not emerge with like force in the Old Testament. Just as true knowledge becomes possible only through revelatory grace, just so the way of perfect righteousness is possible only by the mercy and with the help of God.[18]

We must ask ourselves another question also: Do the Old Testament and the late Jewish texts speak also of the perfection of *God?* God himself is never given this attribute directly, no doubt for the intrinsic reason that with God no defect in his nature is possible, so that the predicate "perfect" becomes for him superfluous and hardly meaningful. But as concerns God's acts, their perfection can be stressed (cf. Deut 32:4). The Lord's precepts are right (Ps 19:8), and to the pious and the just the perfection of God's works stands revealed. In Psalm 18, in which David looks back upon his life (an almost exact parallel to 2 Samuel 22), the psalmist says: "With the loyal thou dost show thyself loyal; with the blameless man thou dost show thyself blameless" (v. 25). The context shows that he is thinking of God's

[18] B. Rigaux, *loc. cit.*, 240 f., indicates three elements as constitutive of Qumran "perfection": a moral element—obedience and following the way; a mystical element—growing out of the purification and the gift of the Holy Spirit; and a "gnostic" element—the knowledge of the divine plan. It would, however, be best to avoid the term "gnostic"; at any rate, the "gnosis" of gnosticism is a different matter.

166

loyal, unfailing help: "This God—his way is perfect; the promise of the Lord proves true; he is a shield for all those who take refuge in him" (v. 30). We hear a faint echo of the thought in the Qumran texts: "The God who girded me with strength and made my way safe" (v. 32). The Qumran community rule, too, speaks of the righteousness of God's ways (1 QS 1:13). And it is further significant that another divine attribute, holiness, is in many passages coupled with "perfect."[19] It might be that the "men of perfect holiness" were thinking of the ordinance in Leviticus (19:2): "You shall be holy; for I the Lord your God am holy."

After these preliminary investigations we now turn to the two passages in Matthew's gospel.

PERFECTION ACCORDING TO THE SERMON ON THE MOUNT

The exhortation that man must be perfect as the heavenly Father is perfect (Mt 5:48) stands at the end of the explanations concerning the duty to love one's enemies. The reference to God's works in verse 45 serves to give natural man a reason for the otherwise incomprehensible and exacting demand. Since God makes his sun to rise on the evil and on the good and sends rain on the just and on the unjust, we, too, ought to love our enemies and pray for those who persecute us if we want to become sons of our heavenly Father.

[19] 1 QS 8:20; Dam 7:4 f.; 20, 2, 5, 7.

167

The concluding exhortation in verse 48 falls into place; it lays still greater stress on the need to imitate God.[20] In Luke's version, the connection is even closer and clearer (6:35 f.). Matthew inserts several sentences on human conduct (5:46 f.). Even the tax collectors love those who love them, even the Gentiles salute their "brethren"—Jesus' disciples must do *more* than that. In Luke, the sequence of the verses is reversed: the reference to God's works is followed immediately by the final exhortation. Most likely this is the original sequence.[21]

But the exhortation is also phrased differently in Luke: "Be merciful, even as your Father is merciful!" (Lk 6:36). This is likely to represent the original wording, although the exegetes are not united on the matter. J. Dupont rightly points out that Luke's "merciful" is far more in harmony with the language of the Bible, since the Old Testament frequently applies *this* attribute

---

[20] Cf. H. J. Schoeps, "Von der imitatio dei zur Nachfolge Christi," in *Aus frühchristlicher Zeit* (Tübingen, 1950), 286–301; R. Schnackenburg, *The Moral Teaching of the New Testament;* A. Schulz, *Nachfolgen und Nachahmen* (Munich, 1962), 226–234.

[21] Thus also J. Dupont, *Les Béatitudes* I (Bruges-Louvain, 1958), 154; the same, "Soyez parfaits" (Mt, V, 48)—"Soyez miséricordieux" (Lc, VI, 36)," in *Sacra Pagina* II (Paris-Gembloux, 1959), 150–162.

to God himself.[22] The word "merciful," further, follows naturally from the description of God's works that has gone before (even though Luke abridges that description), and is in harmony with what Jesus himself says about God; we need think only of the parable of the prodigal son, the unmerciful servant, or the laborers in the vineyard. Matthew has changed "merciful" intentionally to "perfect." What may have been his motives? First of all, probably the intention to stress more strongly the attitude expected of a *disciple;* for, as we have seen, "perfect" is a quality for which man must strive, while it can hardly be applied to God.

There is a further observation. There is a good reason why Matthew has inserted those sentences —on the love and kindness which all men, even tax collectors and Gentiles, show to their likes— between the statements about God's works and his exhortation to perfection. "If you love those who those who love you—do not even the tax collectors do the same?" This turn of phrase, found only in Matthew, reminds us of the programmatic sentence with which all the antitheses of the Sermon on the Mount are introduced: "Unless your righteousness exceeds that of the scribes and Pharisees, you will never enter the kingdom of heaven" (Mt 5:20). In Matthew's version, the

[22] J. Dupont in *Sacra Pagina* II, 154 ff., with many OT references.

Preacher on the Mount demands a greater justice, one that exceeds the Jewish aspiration. This moral endeavor expected from the aspirants to God's kingdom, which goes far beyond prevailing standards, is the subject of all the antitheses and reaches its climax in the commandment to love one's enemies. Here, the "excess" over the legally oriented morality of the Pharisees is to be highlighted once more—in the light of God's paradoxical behavior. This attitude, which is focused on God's own holiness, Matthew sums up at the climactic end of the antitheses in the concept of "perfection." Matthew does not intend that perfection shall consist *only* in love of one's enemies; he merely uses this extreme case to reach the all-encompassing conclusion: "You therefore must be perfect, as your heavenly Father is perfect!" That man is perfect who belongs exclusively and completely to God, and who desires nothing else than to do God's will totally, so that he may enter into God's kingdom.

And finally, there is one more reason for Matthew's formulation of the sentence. We have noted repeatedly that the first evangelist, of Judeo-Christian background, was probably influenced by Leviticus 19:2, which reads: "You shall be holy; for I the Lord your God am holy." It can be shown that Matthew (probably following a Jewish tradition) combines the decalogue and the law of holiness, and weaves both into his paraenesis which is designed for the instruction of the members of the early Church.[23] In Matthew 19:18 f., too, the prescriptions of the decalogue are followed by the commandment to love one's neighbor, in accordance with Leviticus 19:18. The antitheses of the Sermon on the Mount not only include statements from the Ten Commandments (cf. Mt 5:21 and 27), but also discuss other instructions from the Pentateuch (Leviticus and Deuteronomy)—e.g., 5:31, 33, and 38—including finally the law of love according to Leviticus 19:18 (Mt 4:43). It seems likely, then, that the evangelist in the final exhortation of Mt 5:48 had in mind that fundamental demand for holiness of Leviticus 19:2. He did not mean merely to repeat that demand, he meant also to exceed it: the holiness demanded in the Old Testament, as the Lord God of Israel is holy, must now prove itself as perfection as the Father in heaven is perfect. This may be no more than a shift in language —but it is not unimportant to the evangelist who is forever intent on underlining what is new, insuperable, definitive in the message and summons of Jesus.

This insight brings us closer to determining the meaning of perfection as Matthew sees it. For him, perfection is an all-embracing term for man's duty—which grows out of Jesus' message of God's kingdom—to show himself worthy of the salvation offered to him, to love God with all his heart,

[23] K. Stendahl, *The School of St. Matthew* (Uppsala, 1954), 136–138.

171

and above all "to seek first his kingdom" (cf. Mt 6:33). This is not the place to explicate Jesus' entire ethic concerning God's kingship.[24] But we may present a few points which throw light on the specific nature of that perfection which the Sermon on the Mount demands of the Christian.

We must first call to mind that Jesus' message is eschatological. Because he proclaims God's kingdom as imminent, indeed as present, palpable, and effective in his own person and works, he therefore demands also a new morality which is in keeping with the time of salvation and thus must also completely "fulfill" the old law (Mt 5:17).[25] Of course this does not yet mean sinlessness, that incorrupt and incorruptible union with God which the saved will possess in the kingdom of God, that change of heart by God's spirit of

[24] Cf. R. Schnackenburg, *The Moral Teaching of the New Testament;* also J. Bonsirven, *Le Règne de Dieu* (Paris, 1957), 80–151; E. Neuhäusler, *Anspruch und Antwort Gottes* (Düsseldorf, 1962).

[25] How to explain in more detail this "fulfill" is a matter of lively discussion; most likely, the thought is of the fulfillment, and more than fulfillment, of God's will as discernible in the Old Testament, by the coming of Jesus. Cf. also H. Ljungman, *Das Gesetz erfüllen* (Lund, 1954); W. Trilling, *Das wahre Israel* (Munich, 1964), 171–179; G. Barth, "Das Gesetzesverständnis des Evangelisten Matthäus," in *Überlieferung und Auslegung im Matthäusevangelium* (Neukirchen, 1960), 60–65; G. Strecker, *Der Weg der Gerechtigkeit* (Göttingen, 1962), 143–147.

which even the prophets spoke;[26] but it is that state of belonging to God, and that brotherhood, which are focused on that vision and motivated by it and which are made possible by the measure of salvation that has already been granted—possible as far as can be on this earth, in this eon. Jesus expects and demands that such a conduct, pointing toward eschatological consummation, be realized in thought and deed. Thus it is justified to define Christian "perfection" as the "way of life reflecting the salvific reality of the eschaton."[27] But we must emphasize that the call to "perfection" is addressed to every Christian; every Christian ought to reflect in his individual and social way of life something of the glory of the eschatological union with God.[28] The demands of the Sermon on the Mount deal after all with life in this world. Jesus addresses the married when he demands married faithfulness down into the recesses of the heart (Mt 5:28), or forbids divorce which until then had been allowed (5:32). It was his intention that the expected eschatological consummation should cast its radiance ahead upon the conditions of the present world and time. Dissension, revenge, and enmity among men were to be extinguished even now; the paralyzing worries of earthly life were to be conquered; and that

[26] Jer 31:33, 32:38–41; Ez 36:25–29; 37:27 f.
[27] W. Hillmann, "Perfectio Evangelica," *Wissenschaft und Weisheit* 19 (1956), 161–172, specifically 165.
[28] *Ibid.*, 167.

173

love of wealth which separates man from God was to be overcome.

But Jesus' message may also be regarded as a restoration of the original order. Such a view does not conflict with the eschatological aspect, since the eschaton is at the same time a *restitutio in integrum* (cf. Acts 3:21, *apokatastasis*).[29] It is true that the antitheses of the Sermon on the Mount are eschatologically motivated in the introductory statement (Mt 5:20): to enter into God's kingdom requires a greater righteousness; but the individual statements are presented as a new interpretation of the divine will, as Jesus' authoritative proclamations ("But I say to you . . ."); and that presupposes that Jesus has knowledge of God's original, uncurtailed, pure, and holy will. There is a telling example of the way in which Jesus understands and justifies his new interpretation of the old divine law, and that is the exchange concerning divorce, which is reported elsewhere than in the Sermon on the Mount (Mk 10:2–9; Mt 19:3–9). In contradiction to the permission

[29] The doctrine of the "restoration" (apokatastasis) must not be understood as the mere return of initiary time (paradise); what is at stake here is rather a surpassing renewal, transcending the old and making all things perfect, a definitive renewal that may thus be called a new creation. Cf. E. L. Dietrich, *Die endzeitliche Wiederherstellung bei den Propheten* (Giessen, 1928); F. Mussner in *LThK* L (1957), 708 f.; G. Schneider, *Neuschöpfung oder Wiederkehr?* (Düsseldorf, 1961).

granted by Moses, which allowed a letter of
divorce, Jesus refers back to Genesis (1:27; 2:24)
and demands that the union of man and wife
which God created in the beginning must not be
dissolved. He thus reduces Moses' command—
which after all was also given in God's name!—to
a relative status, to a concession limited in time
and made "for your hardness of heart"; but now
he demands that God's original will be obeyed
completely. The reasons given for the love of
one's enemies go in a slightly different direction,
but come down to the same: because God is kind
and merciful to all men without exception, including the evil and the unjust, therefore Jesus'
disciples are to follow God's example and imitate
his absolute and holy nature, without regard to
their human emotions and inner reluctance. This
thought is combined with the eschatological motivation; in this way, the disciples are to become
the sons of the heavenly Father (Mt 5:45a; Lk
6:35c). What is meant is not that they are to become like God here and now; rather, the promise
that men "shall be called sons of God" speaks of
a gift to be bestowed in the kingdom of God to
come, and Luke's version adds further: "Your
reward will be great" (Lk 6:35b). The primary
and closest motivation for love of one's enemies,
however, is the example of the heavenly Father,
who acts in just that way and thus points the way
to the disciples. We might also say: Jesus leads
men once again back to an immediate relation to
God, in which they experience God's will in its

purity, complete, and are to become "perfect" by doing God's will.[30] "To be perfect as your heavenly Father is perfect" also means: "because your heavenly Father is perfect" and demands such an attitude from you.

Here we must not overlook an aspect which is inherent in Jesus' whole message of salvation, and also underlies the demands of the Sermon on the Mount. It is: The new eschatological and primally pure morality of Jesus' disciples, the undivided surrender to God, and the unlimited love of brother become possible only by God's anticipatory love and by his present work of salvation. Perfection is not only a requirement, it is a gift as well: it is man's answer to God's work which makes man capable of perfection. God's anticipatory love is best illustrated by the parable of the unmerciful servant (Mt 18:23—35). That servant had experienced unmatched forbearance from his master, who had expected him to show forbearance to his fellow servant in turn; when he fails, the master rightly reproves him: "Should not you have had mercy on your fellow servant, as I had mercy on you?" (v. 33). Overwhelmed by God's love, we are to return supreme love. God asks nothing from us which he has not first given to us in incomparably richer measure. The capac-

[30] Cf. H. Schürman, "Eschatologie und Liebesdienst in der Verkündung Jesu," in *Kaufet die Zeit aus!* (Paderborn, 1959), 39–71; E. Neuhäusler, *loc. cit.* 43–97, esp. 45–52.

ity for perfection is not stated directly in the Sermon on the Mount, but it is given, proclaimed implicitly, simply in the manner in which Jesus speaks to his disciples of the Father. In the "Our Father" (Mt 6:9–13) he teaches them to talk to God like his children,[31] and in the discourse on needless anxiousness (6:25–32) he teaches them to trust in him as children do. The important exhortation to prayer of petition (7:711) encourages them to lay before God everything that concerns their discipleship, their efforts, and their tasks in behalf of God's kingdom: God, in the love and power of his nature, is even more eager and more capable than our fathers on earth to do "good" (Luke has "give the Holy Spirit") to those who pray for it. This is at least an allusion that all strength for his work, and for his moral endeavor, comes to Jesus' disciple from the Father.

Now we are in a position to distinguish the "perfection" called for in the Sermon on the Mount from that idea of perfection which dominates us all as heirs of Greek thought. That perfection is not an ideal which we are to approach step by step, without ever reaching it; rather, it is a total surrender to God which we as Christ's disciples must perform, and by which we are to

---

[31] To "abba," cf. G. Kittel in *ThWNT* I, 4–6; J. Jeremias in *Synoptische Studien* (*Festschrift für A. Wilkenhauser*) (Munich, 1954), 86–89, and *The Central Message of the New Testament* (London, 1965) 9–30; G. Schrenk in *ThWNT* V, 984 f.

structure our life in the world, each according to his vocation. It is the love of God with all our heart and all our strength, the love from which grows also our love of neighbor and of our most distant brothers, of friend and enemy, in the image of God's love. Nor is this perfection inspired by a humanism which is striving for a fully rounded humanity, with all its powers developed to perfection—it is a life in the sight and in the company of God, so that we may pass muster before him, however miserable our humanity may still remain. Finally, that perfection is not an ethical blueprint but a religious demand: the demand to submit and surrender to the eternally superior God in obedience to his call, in the resolve to be pure in heart and radical in deed, and also in reliance on his mercy, help, and salvation.

Matthew described this inner attitude in conscious contrast to the legal-minded piety of Pharisees and scribes which fails to realize the will of God, and closes rather than opens the kingdom of God to mankind (cf. Mt 23:13).[32] He employed the Jewish terminology which is found already in the Old Testament, and tried to show what is

---

[32] Cf. E. Haenchen, "Matthäus 23," *Zeitschrift für Theologie und Kirche* 48 (1951), 38–63; W. Trilling, *Das wahre Israel*, 198–201; R. Hummel, *Die Auseinandersetzung zwischen Kirche und Judentum im Matthäusevangelium* (Munich, 1963), assumes a Judeo-Christian character of Matthew's Church, but with anti-Pharisee propaganda.

the true "justice" and "perfection" demanded by Jesus. Luke, addressing a formerly pagan audience, interprets Jesus' eschatological message and demand differently, and yet he teaches the same thing. Immediately after the blessings and the cries of woe, he leads off with the challenging demand to love one's enemies—and never allows his audience to escape again from this grasp with which God grips the whole man. For him, there was no reason to depart from the original wording. On the contrary, he would welcome the demand: "Be merciful, even as your Father is merciful!"

PERFECTION AND THE IMITATION OF CHRIST: THE EVANGELIC COUNSELS

The second passage in which Matthew (and only he) uses the expression "perfect" leads us still more deeply into our complex of questions. Differing from the Sermon on the Mount, Jesus' demand is addressed this time not to all men, but only to the "rich young man" (Mt 19:21). Further, Jesus' twofold answer seems to imply also a twofold demand: the keeping of the commandments is (seemingly) just a preliminary step, and only the surrender of all possessions constitutes real perfection. Finally, and this is the most important point, perfection is tied very closely to the imitation of Jesus. We shall for the moment leave aside the problem of the "evangelic counsels" which have long troubled the treatment of this pericope.

We shall start again by trying to throw some light on the procedure and intentions of the first evangelist in giving to his account a special structure and formulation differing from Mark (and from Luke who here follows Mark very closely). According to Mark 10:17–22, Jesus replies to the man's question, "What must I do to inherit eternal life?" with the reminder ("You know . . .") of the Ten Commandments, and enumerates the second tablet, in an unusual sequence.[33] To the man's answer, "Teacher, all these I have observed from my youth," Jesus says: "You lack one thing; go, sell what you have, and give to the poor, and you will have treasure in heaven; and come, follow me!" Numerous observations prove that Matthew had Mark's report before him and consciously altered it.[34] The divergences significant for our purpose are these: *1.* Jesus' first answer is expanded: "If you would enter life, keep the commandments!" And only after the man asks "Which?" in return, does Jesus enumerate them. *2.* The law of love from Leviticus 19:18 is added to the selection from the decalogue. *3.* The "young man" asks of his own accord: "What do I still lack?" *4.* Jesus' further answer runs: "If you would be perfect, go, sell what you possess. . . ."

[33] Probably the intention was to list first the prohibitions, and after them the positive commandment to care for one's parents.

[34] Cf. J. Schmid, *Das Evangelium nach Matthäus* (Regensburg, 1956), 281 f.; J. Levie in *La formation des Évangiles* (Louvain, 1957), 45.

The fact that our starting point is the Sermon on the Mount will facilitate our understanding of the evangelist's intention with this pericope. We have pointed out above that in both instances the examples from the decalogue are followed by the law of love (cf. the second alteration). Matthew did not at all wish to see the Old Testament law abrogated, even after the Sermon on the Mount; on the contrary, he underlined its validity and binding force (cf. 5:17–19); this is why he now lays stress also on Jesus' first reply to the young man (cf. the first alteration). But he also interprets Jesus' Sermon on the Mount in the sense that the law has to be fulfilled and exceeded in a new way; this is why he ended the antitheses with the formulation: "Therefore be perfect . . .!"; this is also why he now includes the same summons to perfection in Jesus' further answer to young man (cf. the fourth alteration).

To gain a still fuller understanding, let us try to imagine what practical catechetical purpose Matthew had in mind with the pericope of the rich young man. We shall make no mistake when we assume that he wanted Judeo-Christians (or Jewish catechumens) to learn from the example of the rich young man what demands Christ made on them in excess of their traditional Jewish law. The fact that the young man is intended as the type of the Jewish aspirant for baptism is possibly revealed in the third alteration, where the young man himself is made to ask: "What do I still lack?" And Jesus, without retracting his first instruction that the young man must keep the commandments, now adds a further demand: In total self-surrender, in complete submission to God (which here takes the concrete expression of giving away his fortune), the young man must enter *Jesus' followership.* This demand explains the peculiar parallelism and dialectic of Jesus' double answer (the first and the fourth alterations): In order to enter into life it is necessary to fulfill God's commandments—in the sense in which Jesus understands fulfillment (cf. the Sermon on the Mount). And yet, considered in a different light, that is not enough, because it could be done in a purely legalistic way (as the young man has perhaps done so far). If he wishes to be "perfect," which means blameless before the law, as God wills him to be, then he must take radical action, here give up his wealth, and follow Jesus.

A few points need to be clarified to substantiate our interpretation. Jesus' double answer cannot refer to two different degrees of moral endeavor to which the inquirer may or may not rise as he wishes, and even less to two different degrees of blessedness he might thereby attain. The matter has been clearly stated by J. Herkenrath.[35] "To enter eternal life" is synonymous with "to enter the kingdom of God," and this is the sole and also the supreme promise which Jesus has to

[35] *Die Ethik Jesu in ihren Grundzügen* (Düsseldorf, 1926), 164 f.

give. " 'Treasure is in heaven' is here not intended
as a special reward (no more than it is in Mark),
but as the recompense for the surrender of worldly
wealth; it thus coincides with 'eternal life' in
Matthew 6:20."[36] The expression "If you *would*
be perfect" leaves it up to the young man whether
to seek perfection or to forego this "higher" resolve; for Jesus' first answer to him uses the same
expression, "If you would enter life . . . ," and confronts him, as is generally recognized, with an
urgent necessity. In Mark's gospel, all doubt is
removed by Jesus' answer: "You lack one thing!"
while in Matthew the same expression is ascribed
to the young man. Thus J. Schmid is right in saying "that the thought in Matthew is the same as
in Mark. Jesus' demand of 'perfection' cannot be
regarded as a mere counsel, since the surrender of
one's possessions to the poor is part of the followership of Jesus (cf. Lk 14:33), that is, is not left
to the decision of the disciple."[37]

We may then draw this conclusion: *For this
man,* Jesus interprets the surrender of his fortune
as the fulfillment of God's commandments the
way he understands them, as the expression of
abandonment to God, of radical obedience—altogether in the sense of the Sermon on the
Mount (cf. Mt 6:24). The same thing is suggested perhaps by the manner in which Jesus
right at the start recites God's commandments to

[36] *Ibid.,* 164.
[37] *Ibid.,* 282.

the young man. In Mark, Jesus follows "Do not bear false witness!" with "Do not defraud!" According to Jewish parallels, this may also mean "Do not withhold just wages!"[38] It is thus possible that Jesus makes this demand in view of the inquirer's wealth. Matthew omits the expression, but after the decalogue adds the law of love, which may here also intend to remind the young man of his particular duties arising from his wealth. While it may be doubtful that Jesus' intent can be immediately gathered from his first answer, his second reply makes it quite clear that he regards it God's inexorable call for this man to separate himself completely from his possessions, and to follow Jesus in poverty. Jesus' demand is of one piece, although it is *revealed* gradually. He who would enter life must be perfect. He must obey God's commandments, but in the way in which Jesus interprets them; in case of the rich young man, it means he must renounce his earthly goods and follow Jesus.

We may now ask how the *Imitation of Jesus* is related to *perfection*. We must remind ourselves that "imitation" or "followership," and "discipleship" have undergone a change of meaning.[39] Originally, "to follow (or imitate) Jesus" meant

---

[38] Cf. Dt 24:14 (A); Mal 3:5; Sir 31:22 after the LXX; James 5:4, 1st verse. Also V. Taylor, *The Gospel According to St. Mark* (London, 1952), 428.

[39] See above, Chapter "The Imitation of Christ," pp. 118–119.

to follow Jesus' call and become his personal disciple. However, in the early Church the concept of "disciple" acquired a wider meaning, clearly shown in the Acts (Chapters 6–11); in the gospel of John, too, all those are "disciples" who join in the faith (cf. 8:12, 31; 12:35 f.). In the evangelist's own comments, the distinction between Jesus' words to his "disciples" in the narrower sense, and his words to the people, is often blurred.[40] There can be no doubt that those demands which stemmed from his message of God's kingdom were addressed by Jesus to all men; but neither can it be doubted that he called only a small number to become his special disciples and give up house and home, family, and profession.

Does this mean that the idea of perfection remains limited to that small number of disciples? The answer is an emphatic "no"; Matthew makes it sufficiently clear in the Sermon on the Mount that every aspirant to God's kingdom ought to be "perfect" (5:48). Accordingly, we may not interpret the second passage in the pericope of the rich young man to mean that "perfection" consisted generally in the surrender of earthly wealth. Jesus' final words to the young man are of course an invitation to him to follow as a "disciple" in the fullest sense: but we must under-

---

[40] This holds especially for the requirement to renounce all property (Mk 10:23–27; Lk 12:13–34), but also for the readiness to suffer (Mk 8:34–38). Cf. Neuhäusler, *loc. cit.,* 170–185.

stand it to mean that, *for this man,* the perfection that is demanded of all men—complete surrender to God—took the specific form of a life in poverty such as it was lived in the community of Jesus' constant followers. Our earlier interpretation is thus confirmed; but we must inquire further. How did the early Church understand Jesus' demand when it extended the "followership of Jesus" to all believers? Doubtless in this way, that the demand for perfection takes concrete form for each and every Christian in and through the imitation of the Lord. If formerly, in the presence and by the decision of Jesus, God's call took on a concrete form for every man, should that not apply in a similar way for later believers? In this light, the "common property" of the Jerusalem community (Acts 2:44 f.; 4:32) becomes more intelligible.[41] It represented the realization of the idea of poverty in the specific circumstances of the original community. Assuming the believers who came after Easter transposed the idea of "followership" into their own situation, applied it to their conditions of life—did they not have to ask themselves what concrete demands the Lord was making on them and on each individual? (cf. Acts 4:36 f.; 5:1–11).

In this light the "evangelic counsels" assume a new complexion. They have a biblical basis, although they have not always been properly

[41] Cf. H.-J. Degenhardt, *Lukas, Evangelium der Armen* (Stuttgart, 1965), 160–174 and excursus 188–207.

based on the Bible. They are God's call to the individual man to enter into Christ's service more firmly than other men who do not hear the call; they are addressed to men who are to be directly and exclusively available for Christ and his work. We cannot here analyze in detail the three classic counsels; we shall show only briefly how poverty, chastity, and obedience fit into this perspective.

The decision of individual men to make themselves eunuchs for the sake of the kingdom of heaven has been accepted by Jesus in Matthew 19:11 f., and obviously been defended against unfriendly critics.[42] They were followers who were moved by Jesus' preachings of God's kingdom to renounce marriage, either from the start or by giving up their existing marriage. The matter has the character of a counsel, since Jesus did not demand it of everybody, not even of all the disciples in the narrower sense; the majority of the "apostles" themselves after Easter do not seem to have given up marriage (cf. 1 Cor 9:5).[43] Jesus approved of that condition, even while he himself led a virginal life. He regarded it as a form of total surrender to God to which such men had been inspired—indeed he regarded it as a special grace of God (cf. v. 11). He seems to have demanded surrender of all property from

[42] Cf. J. Blinzler, "Εἰδὶν εὐνοῦχοι," ZNW 48 (1957), 254–270, particularly 257–259.
[43] Cf. J. B. Bauer, "*Uxores Circumducere* (1 Cor 9:5) *BZ* NF 3 (1959), 54–102.

all those who wanted to share permanently his
wandering life (cf. Mk 10:28–30; Lk 14:33). In
this respect, the counsel of poverty is far more
compelling.

The counsel of obedience is least clearly expressed in the gospels, because it was added later
and became the principal mark of the monastic
life. Its biblical foundation would seem to be
Jesus' repeated call to service. "Whoever would
be great among you must be your servant, and
whoever would be first among you must be slave
of all!" (Mk 10:43). When Luke shifts the disciples' quarrel over their rank to the scene of the
Last Supper, and emphasizes Jesus' service at the
table (22:26 f.), he surely had the conditions of
the later communities in mind. John underlines
still more the example of Jesus in his description
of the footwashing (13:1–5). The disciples' obedience to Jesus and to God lies as such on a different plane. But if we consider that the group of
disciples around Jesus, with its distinctive ways
of life, could become a paradigm for later believers, we can also understand as an extension
of the biblical example St. Benedict's thought that
in the monastic family the abbot represents Christ
himself, and that obedience shown to him is as
good as obedience to Christ himself.[44]

The insight that every Christian has the duty
to be perfect, and is called to realize his perfec-

[44] Cf. E. M. Heufelder, *Die Evangelischen Räte* (Vienna, 1953), 31–42.

tion concretely in the imitation of Jesus, yields an important consequence for the believers living in the world. Although they have not heard the call to lead a life apart, in the manner of the original disciples, they have been called nonetheless to seek for concrete ways in which they may attain perfection. For them, too, Jesus' demands in the Sermon on the Mount are not just a distant and unattainable ideal, nor are they of concern only to the priesthood, but are demands addressed to them as well. In their earthly station and profession they, too, are called to attempt total surrender and the radical striving for God's kingdom. And here again, the primary commandment of love points the way: by loving their brothers, their neighbors, and their enemies, they must strive to meet Jesus' demand: "You, therefore, must be perfect, as your heavenly Father is perfect!"

VII

The Concept of the World in the New Testament

Throughout the New Testament there predominates an idea of the world that provokes modern man to objections. The "world" or "this world" appears in such a pessimistic light that the man of the twentieth century—at home on this earth and ready to conquer the spaces beyond it, in possession of the earth's riches and in love with its beauty—can only shake his head in wonderment. In James 4:4, for instance, we read: "Friendship with the world is enmity with God; therefore whoever wishes to be a friend of the world makes himself an enemy of God." To modern man, such an hostility toward the world belongs to a time when man, oppressed by anxiety for his bare existence and confused by false and life-denying ideals, tried to escape from earthly reality and sought refuge in an imaginary "heaven." For modern man, these times are over and done with; today's world is for him an arena of action full of untapped, indeed inexhaustible possibilities, and all he needs to do is use his own powers, develop science and technology, plan with economic and political wisdom, and try to keep peace among the nations. Such statements of the Bible seem to him unrewarding, and so he turns aside and leaves it to the stunted specimens among his contemporaries to reject our world, and to hope for a better one.

This view is due to a profound misunderstanding, a failure to come to grips with what the Bible says and means. The situation is like that with the biblical account of the creation of the world: the Bible does not propose to give a scientific description, but to state what is important for man's salvation. In the same way, its statements about the "world" do not concern the earth as the arena of human life and activity; they do not intend to hamper man in his endeavors to understand and subdue the forces of nature, to improve earthly conditions as far as possible, and to bring about a better future. Instead, the Bible wants to teach man something about his conduct in the existing world, about his moral attitude, and to show him how to find the right way in his dealings with others and with the things of the world, in his striving for personal fulfillment. The point is thus not how to shape the outward conditions on earth, but how to put order into man's personal life. The "world," in this perspective, is not the visible and investigatable universe, not this earth and the potentials slumbering within it, nor even mankind as a demonstrable magnitude and power potential; it is rather a spiritual state of affairs which derives from man's personal attitude toward the things and fellow men, the historical circumstances and influences, that surround him. Only when we see man as a being who pursues a purposeful existence in the constant confrontation with the world around him, a being constantly striving to achieve an understanding of himself—only then do we catch a glimpse of what the New Testament wants to say with its statements about "world." We hear a faint, diluted echo of what is meant here, in the expression "world view"—and even today no thoughtful man, however far from religious he may be, can do without some world view.

However, the concept of world in the New Testament is incapable of a clear and unequivocal definition, for it has many layers; besides, it differs in the various writings. Space does not allow us to trace the diverse shadings, and to study the various concepts in the synoptic gospels, in Paul, John, the late Letters, and the Apocalypse.[1] In-

[1] Literature: H. Sasse in *ThWNT* I (1933), 197–209; III (1938), 882–896; R. Löwe, *Kosmos und Aion* (Gütersloh, 1935); G. Bornkamm, "Christus und die Welt in der urchristlichen Botschaft," *Gesammelte Aufsätze* I (Munich, 1958), 157–172; R. Völkl, *Christ und Welt nach dem Neuen Testament* (Würzburg, 1961), an inclusive presentation, with a rich bibliography; N. Brox, article *Welt* in *Handbuch Theologischer Grundbegriffe*, ed. H. Fries (Munich, 1963), II, 813–822; G. von Rad, "Aspekte alttestamentlichen Weltverständnisses," *Evangelische Theo-*

stead, we shall concentrate here on a meaning of
"world" which more or less pervades all New
Testament writings, and which is connected with
a general spiritual current of those days called
dualism.[2] The pessimistic view of the world—too

logie 24 (1964), 57–73; G. Johnston, "Οἰκουμένη und
κόδμος in the New Testament," *New Testament Studies* 10 (1963/64), 352–360; W. Schrage, "Die Stellung
zur Welt bei Paulus, Epiktet und in der Apoka-
lyptik," *Zeitschrift für Theologie und Kirche* 61
(1964), 125–154; H. Schlier, "Welt und Mensch nach
dem Johannesevangelium," in *Besinnung auf das
Neue Testament* (Freiburg, 1964), 242–253.

[2] Because this general label is applied to a manner of
thinking that moves within contrasting concepts, one
must be careful to distinguish clearly the given
variety and the underlying ideas and motivations.
Many classifications have been attempted, and dual-
isms of a metaphysical, cosmic, anthropological, sal-
vationist, and moral character have been discerned;
but the transitions are often very fluid. For the New
Testament, the background of Jewish dualism is particularly significant, and for some parties (Paul,
John) more precisely the dualism that expresses itself
in the Qumran writings; gnostic dualism is instructive in showing the limits that are set to belief in
Christ. Cf. H. Jonas, *Gnosis und spätantiker Geist* I
(Göttingen, 1934); on the concept of *kosmos,* pp.
146–156; S. Pétrement, *Le dualism chez Platon, les
Gnostiques et les Manichéens* (Paris, 1947); S. Aalen,
*Die Begriffe "Licht" und "Finsternis" im Alten Testa-
ment, im Spätjudentum und im Rabbinismus* (Oslo,
1951); F. Nötscher, *Zur Theologischen Terminologie*

pessimistic, perhaps, in our opinion—is the price which the New Testament must pay for being the work of human beings living in history and involved in their times; but it does not mean that the New Testament is sold on that mental attitude. We will have to watch for the differences between the "dualistic" thought of the New Testament and the thought of the world around it, and for the ways in which a purely negative attitude, a flight into a "heavenly" or "future" world, is overcome. Beyond that, we must uncover strata of thought which are concealed under those outwardly dominating statements about "world," but are nonetheless present throughout—although most often not under the *term* "world"—and will allow an altogether different "world view" once they are exposed. After we have thus placed before us two groups of statements and the tension between them, we must inquire what their meaning is for our present Christian understanding of human life, and for our concrete conduct in the historical situation of today.

der Qumran-Texte (Bonn, 1956), 70–133; U. Bianchi, *Il dualismo religioso* (Rome, 1958); H. W. Huppenbauer, *Der Mensch zwischen zwei Welten. Der Dualismus der Texte von Qumran* (Zurich, 1959); H. Dörrie and J. Duchesne-Guillemin, *"Dualismus,"* in *Reallexikon für Antike und Christentum,* IV (Stuttgart, 1959), 334–350; O. Böcher, *Der johanneische Dualismus im Zusammenhang des nachbiblischen Judentums* (Gütersloh, 1965).

THE HISTORICALLY DECAYED AND
MORALLY CORRUPT WORLD

In order to understand the dark and pessimistic statements of the New Testament concerning the world, we must take a clear look at the Hellenistic period in which Christianity arose, with its tendencies to take a somber view of this world. Among the Jews, the religion of the Old Testament—originally full of the joy of creation and the affirmation of life—was overshadowed, after severe national catastrophes and great suppression, by melancholy thoughts that show the influence of Iranian dualism. The present times were regarded as evil, and thus men turned their eyes with greater longing toward a bright future. The banishment from the holy land of the fathers provided the soil upon which an eschatological hope could grow which took ever more "apocalyptic" forms. By this we mean a certain religiously determined view of history, according to which the present world is under the dominion of evil; but by God's design it will be replaced—after periods of mounting wickedness and horror—by the future world of salvation and glory. When the wickedness of men, and the horrors which the just and the select must suffer, have reached their peak, then God will intervene, destroy the present world, hold judgment, and bring about a new and better world.[3] In his investigation of the roots

[3] On Jewish apocalyptic, we may cite only the following basic works: P. Volz, *Die Eschatologie der jüdi-*

of the apocalyptic world view, O. Plöger writes: "Thus, with the transformation of the ancient people of Israel into a community of Yahweh, the conditions seem to be present which would with necessity entail the transmutation of the eschatology of the prophets into an apocalyptic view of the future."[4] Again according to Plöger, the eschatologically oriented circles in exile must have offered the soft spot through which alien ideas (those Iranian ideas of a kingdom of evil, a constant battle between good and evil, a final decision) could enter. The apocalyptic eschatology expresses the hope for the future of a community which knew that it was absolutely cut off from the ways of life of the rest of humanity, and which lived in the firm belief that "the nature of this world perishes." These thoughts were not limited to esoteric circles; they invaded even the "official" Judaism guided by devotion to the Torah, even the circles of the scribes and the "brotherhood" of the Pharisees which at the time of Jesus

schen Gemeinde im neutestamentlichen Zeitalter (Tübingen, 1934); H. H. Rowley, *The Relevance of Apocalyptic* (London, 1947); J. Bloch, *On the Apocalyptic in Judaism* (Philadelphia, 1952); S. B. Frost, *Old Testament Apocalyptic, its Origin and Growth* (London, 1952); O. Plöger, *Theokratie und Eschatologie* (Neukirchen, 1959); D. S. Russell, *The Method and Message of Jewish Apocalyptic* (London, 1964), with excellent bibliography.

[4] *Loc. cit.*, 64.

had great influence among the people.[5] The gospels themselves speak not only of the Pharisees' belief in the resurrection, a belief denied by the Sadducees but affirmed by Jesus (Mk 12:18–27), but of the question of the time when God's kingdom will come—a question which Jesus did not, however, answer in the apocalyptic sense (Lk 17:20 f.). Thus we can hardly doubt that Jesus himself represented the apocalyptic hope in the widest sense: a living hope of an imminent future when God himself would reverse the sin, distress, and misery of the present world and bring his kingdom of glory. Jesus was averse only to those narrower, humanly constricted apocalyptic views that we encounter in the typical apocalypses (parts of the Book of Henoch, 4 Ezra, the Baruch Apocalypse): those calculations of the time periods and the exact moment of the end, the elaborate descriptions of terror, the final judgment, the resurrection, and the heavenly world of the future. Against all this, Jesus represented the absolute sovereignty of God, who will not tolerate man to

[5] Various mistaken views prevail concerning the Pharisees, whose origins are still not fully clarified. For a correct understanding see especially J. Jeremias, *Jerusalem zur Zeit Jesu* (Göttingen, 1958), II B, 115–140; W. Beilner, "Der Ursprung des Pharisäismus," *Biblische Zeitschrift* 3 (1959), 235–251; K. Schubert, "Die jüdischen Religionsparteien im Zeitalter Jesu," in *Der historische Jesus und der Christus unseres Glaubens* (Vienna, 1962), 15–101, specifically 57–80.

peep into God's plan of salvation and God's secrets, and does not expect from man fantastic speculations about the future, but faithful service here and now, and boundless confidence.[6]

While we need not here trace further the spiritual situation and religious mood of the Jews at that time, we must realize that the language of the New Testament, and even of the gospels, took from them a peculiar coloring. Some things are indeed clearly recognizable accretions, for example the (in our context) especially important so-called doctrine of the two eons. The Greek word αἰών (a long time, period, age) best renders the Hebrew "world"-concept ʿolam, since that concept is referred to time, not space, in keeping with Semitic thought, tempered by action and by history. In later Judaism, especially in the apocalyptic literature but also in rabbinism, the "present eon" was distinguished from the "coming (future) eon" which God would bring about.[7] A comparison of the synoptic texts shows that Jesus probably did not use these expressions; in the logion of the "hundredfold reward," the distinction of Mark 10:30 (as well as Luke 18:30, while Matthew 19:29 differs) is inserted; the communi-

6 Cf. R. Schnackenburg, *God's Rule and Kingdom* (Freiburg, 1965); E. Neuhäuser, *Anspruch und Antwort Gottes* (Düsseldorf, 1962).

7 Cf. especially the long excursus by P. Billerbeck, *Kommentar zum Neuen Testament aus Talmud und Midrash* IV (Munich, 1928), 799–976; also G. Dalman, *Die Worte Jesu* I (Leipzig, 1930), 120–127.

ties of that time were speaking even then of a present reward for discipleship, and merely reserved the full reward of "eternal life"—which was the reward Jesus had in mind—for the future eon.[8] This usage, of "this" or the "coming eon," is found elsewhere in the New Testament, especially in Paul's Letters.[9] Many passages which speak of the "world" or "this world" mean in fact nothing else than "this eon" which is under the dominion of evil.

Some passages from the New Testament will illustrate the point. God has "made foolish the wisdom of the world" (1 Cor 1:20); Christians have received "not the spirit of the world, but the Spirit which is from God" (1 Cor 2:12). They live in a time of great temptations; for to them has

---

[8] Cf. J. Schmid, *Das Evangelium nach Markus* (Regensburg, 1954), 197 f.; W. Pesch, *Der Lohngedanke in der Lehre Jesu* (Munich, 1955), 70–73, who sees the reward here on earth in the fact that those who follow Jesus, do, in a certain way, share the new life with God already here on earth (p. 72).

[9] "This age": Rom 12:2; 1 Cor 1:20; 2:6, 8; 3:18; 2 Cor 4:4; Eph 1:21; cf. Gal 1:4; "this present world": 1 Tim 6:17; 2 Tim 4:10; Tit 2:12. The "age which is to come" is mentioned only in Eph 1:21; cf. Eph 2:7, "in the coming ages." This is certainly not an accidental formulation, since for Paul the expected time of salvation has already begun in Christ. The "eon to come" is referred to again in Hebrews 6:4, but in the sense that the Christians have already tasted "the powers of the age to come."

come "the end of the ages" (1 Cor 10:11). "This world" is passing away (1 Cor 7:31; cf. 1 Jn 2:17). To Paul (and to every Christian) "the world has been crucified" through Christ, and he (Paul and every Christian) to the world (Gal 6:14). Similarly, the concept of the eon is employed in rejecting "the wisdom of this age" and the doomed "rulers of this age" (1 Cor 2:6, cf. 1:20; 3:18), and to make the positive assertion that Christ wanted "to deliver us from the present evil age" (Gal 1:4). The Christians are warned "not to be conformed to this world" (Rom 12:2). What makes the "world" or "this eon" especially dangerous is that Satan and the demonic powers under his command wield their influence, and are in fact the real rulers wherever Christ's blessed dominion is not yet in effect (cf. 2 Cor 4:4; Eph 2:2; 6:12; Jn 12:31). The "ruler of the world" has, of course, been "cast out" and "judged" by Christ's triumph on the cross (Jn 12:31; 16:11); but this dethronement profits only those who believe in Christ and are united with him. As long as Christ's victory is not all-embracing, it still holds that "the whole world is in the power of the evil one" (1 Jn 5:19). Thus it would be dangerous "to love the world or the things in the world" (1 Jn 2:15).

Despite all these external similarities, however, the Jewish doctrine of the two eons has not been simply carried over, but has been retained only as a form of expression. In fact—and this is an insight of decisive importance—the Christian belongs to the future eon already during the present eon, because he has attained a new existence in Christ. This is expressed most clearly in Paul's statement: "If any one is in Christ, he is a new creation; the old has passed away, behold, the new has come" (2 Cor 5:17). The thought that Christ in his essential nature belongs to God's world of glory finds expression in many and varied ways. "Our commonwealth is in heaven" (Phil 3:20); "For you have died, and your life is hid with Christ in God" (Col 3:3). John speaks of victory already won over the "world": "In the world you have tribulation; but be of good cheer, I have overcome the world" (Jn 16:33); "This is the victory that overcomes the world, our faith" (1 Jn 5:4). And the Letter to the Hebrews speaks of those who have "tasted" the powers of the age to come (6:4 f.).

This consciousness of possessing eschatological salvation even in this world, this eon (though only in an interim, preliminary way) is what constitutes a clear dividing line between Christianity and Judaism. Even the Qumran community, with all its conviction of being the elect and all its certainty of God's nearness and help, still places true salvation into the future.[10] Though the Spirit of

[10] Cf. R. Mayer and J. Reuss, *Die Qumranfunde und die Bibel* (Regensburg, 1959), 153; F. M. Cross, Jr., *The Ancient Library of Qumran and Modern Biblical Studies* (London, 1958), 183 ("All this is to say that what distinguishes the two communities is the 'event' of Jesus as the Christ, his exaltation, his

God illumines the members of the community, purifies and strengthens them, though the community itself seems to be filled with the Spirit: this is not yet the eschatological outpouring of the Spirit of which the Christian community is certain; it is not yet that gift of the divine Spirit which every Christian received in baptism and which determines his life.[11] This inner conquest

resurrection, and the gift of his Spirit."). A different result is reached by the recent and careful study of H.-W. Kuhn, *Enderwartung und Gegenwärtiges Heil* (Göttingen, 1966). He demonstrates by means of four songs from the roll of hymns (hodajoth) that eschatological acts and conditions are already taken into the present (cf. 113–117). The priests' view of their own role, and the "symbolism of the temple" led to the claim of God's salvific presence in the community (138). But Kuhn also underlines: "It is otherwise with Jesus: the proclamation of the presence of God's kingdom is based on Jesus' claim that God's kingship is established *in Jesus' actions*"; the early Christian community distinguishes itself from the Qumran community most strikingly by the *christological* grounds for the salvific presence in the community (204).

[11] Cf. J. Schreiner, "Geistesbegabung in der Gemeinde von Qumran," *BZ* 9 (1965), 161–180; different H.-W. Kuhn, *loc. cit.,* 130–136, who, on the basis of hymn texts, considers it proven that admission to the community brought with it the gift of the divine Spirit. He, too, is critical, however, of the question whether this gift of the Spirit could be understood as an *eschatological* event (136–139).

of Jewish dualism stems from the faith in Jesus Christ as the messiah who has come, who after his death and by his resurrection has entered into the heavenly world, and who lets those who are united with him share in his resurrected life. "The Spirit of him who raised Jesus from the dead dwells in you, he who raised Christ Jesus from the dead will give life to your mortal bodies also" (Rom 8:11). The expectation of a future messiah on the one hand, the faith in a savior who has already come, on the other: this is what divided Judaism and Christianity.

This Christian faith does not do away with the evaluation of this world as sorrowful and evil; yet the world's darkness loses much of its oppressiveness, since the circle of disaster has been broken and a vista opened toward an incorrupt and better world. For the Christian, the world has become a world delivered, even though we are for the present still "groaning" in expectation of the glorious liberty of the children of God, and the whole creation is groaning with us in travail together (Rom 8:21 f.). The author of the First Letter of John writes: "He who is in you is greater that he who is in the world" (4:4). The significance to us of this faith in a forever greater God, who keeps the darkness and evil of this world at bay and lets us share even now in his light and joy, will become fully clear if we compare it with that dualism which we encounter in the pagan-Hellenistic world surrounding the early Church. That world believes in the compelling power of fate, and regards the whole material world as corrupt and evil. Contempt for matter and for the body spreads in many forms, while man attempts to rise from the "lower" world into the higher world of light and life. This view of the world crystallizes especially in gnosticism; man's yearning for deliverance takes this form, that he attempts to free himself from the illusion of the senses and the power of fate by a knowledge of his true self, his spiritual essence. The gnostic emissary—a mythical redeemer who ultimately embodies the self-discovering soul—is sent from the realm of heavenly light down to earth. The description of the lower world is worth noting: "Go into the world of darkness which is filled with wickedness. It is totally filled with wickedness, full of devouring fire. Go to the world of confusion and turmoil without firmness, the world of darkness without a ray of light, the world of persecution and death without life in eternity!"[12] The Book of the Dead of the Mandaeans praises the soul which has left the world: "You have left corruption and the stinking body in which you dwelled, the abode, the abode of evil, the place that is nothing but sin, the world of darkness, hatred, jealousy and strife. . . ."[13]

[12] *Ginza. "Der Schatz" oder "Das grosse Buch der Mandäer,"* translated and annotated by M. Lidzbarski (Göttingen-Leipzig, 1925), 33, 3–7.

[13] *Ginza,* 511, 8 ff.; *Mandäische Liturgien,* ed. M. Lidzbarski (Berlin, 1920), 159.

We are faced here with a radical contempt for
the earthly-material world, a disdain of the life of
the body, a hatred of the body, which attained
a wider influence in Manicheism and, it must be
admitted, in the thought of the Church as well.
Surviving as an undercurrent and occasionally
coming to the surface in various sects, this view
has retained its effects throughout the Middle
Ages and into the present. Nonetheless it is a
regrettable mistake and false development, which
has nothing to do with biblical faith, and which in
places found strong resistance within the early
Church. The pastoral letters reject such false doctrines as "the pretensions of liars whose con-
sciences are seared, who forbid marriage and
enjoin abstinence from foods which God created to be received with thanksgiving by those
who believe and know the truth. For everything
created by God is good, and nothing is to be
rejected if it is received with thanksgiving" (1
Tim 4:2 ff.). In its rejection of unhealthy doctrines
of contempt for the body, the early Church is
mindful of that fundamental truth which it has
taken over from Judaism: God is the creator of
the world and all things in it, and therefore also
the creator of material goods and of the body.
In the unifying view of the Bible, man has only
one bodily existence which he must not deny or
oppose; thus the belief in bodily resurrection is
an integral part of the Christian hope of salvation. But behind the gnostic and related dualistic
thought there is ultimately the idea, not always

clearly expressed, of two arch-principles which are at war from the beginning and forever: good and evil, spirit and matter. This view reduces the value of the visible world on principle, or makes it demonic. The Mandaeans are convinced that "this world has not been created according with the desire of life. . . . This world has been created by the trespasses (of the planets), and the planets stand there, resting upon the treasures of their souls, and lead mankind into sin."[14] In the book of the Mandaean prophet John, the idea is expressed by the image of two kings: "There were *two* kings; *two* natures were created: one king of this world, and one king beyond the worlds. The king of these eons put on a sword and a crown of darkness . . . the king of beyond the worlds placed on his head a crown of light."[15] "World" is the same as darkness; this is one of the "fundamental symbolic equations" of gnosticism.[16] If we consider that the Greeks originally regarded world, the cosmos, as the orderly structure and inherent harmony of the universe, we will become aware of the enormous changes in Greek thought that came about during the Hellenistic period, by reading sentences such as the following in the hermetic writings ("hermetic" in honor of the Greek god Hermes, originally the Egyptian Thoth): "The world is the

---

[14] *Ginza*, 247, 11–15.

[15] *Das Johannesbuch der Mandäer*, ed. M. Lidzbarski (Giessen, 1915), 55.

[16] H. Jonas, *loc. cit.*, 103.

fullness of wickedness, but God (the fullness) of goodness."[17] Such a statement is simply impossible in a (Jewish and) Christian setting, because the world, despite all its historic bondage to evil, always remains God's creation, and thus can never become the very essence of evil.

At this point we are confronted with the question of the meaning and significance of those ardent warnings in the New Testament against the world, and of the pessimistic world view adopted from the age. Why does God's eschatological revelation not take its start from Ancient Israel's world view—open acceptance of the world and joy in the good things of life (possessions, marriage, many children, a long life)? Why is it placed against the background of a somber and melancholy world view? Many reasons may be suggested; without, however, yielding final certainty. Under the surface of Old Israel's optimistic world view, there too we find the consciousness of mankind's historical apostasy from God's order and law. The older (Yahvistic) view of history, in whose account the creation of paradise and of man is quickly followed by man's fall and the rapidly growing sinfulness of mankind leading to the catastrophe of the Great Flood, reveals the knowledge of man's ancient

---

[17] *Corpus Hermeticum* VI, 4, ed. A. D. Nock and A.-J. Festugière (Paris, 1945), I, 74 and 76 f. note. The view here intended does not differ much from a statement such as 1 Jn 5:19: "The whole world is in the power of the evil one."

moral failure as clearly as does the later, priestly report which now stands at the beginning of the Bible in Genesis 1. In that older account we read the grim words: "The Lord saw that the wickedness of man was great, and that every imagination of the thoughts of his heart was only evil continually. And the Lord was sorry that he had made man on the earth, and it grieved him to his heart" (Gen 6:5 f.). And after the report of the Flood, we read: "I will never again curse the ground because of man, for the imagination of man's heart is evil from his youth" (Gen 8:21). But the priestly report, too, which repeatedly stresses that "God saw that it was good," and in the end even "God saw everything that he had made, and behold, it was very good" (Gen 1:31), tells of the flood and remarks: "God saw the earth, and behold, it was corrupt; for all flesh had corrupted their way upon the earth" (Gen 6:12). Evil is a reality in the world and in the history of human kind as long as there has been a "history." Historic life begins with man's activity, and man's activity has never been anything but divided against itself, vacillating between good and evil. The books of revelation of the Old Covenant know it well, and are intended to keep God from being held responsible for it; this is the aspect of "theodicy" in which we must understand the story of man's fall.[18]

[18] Cf. N. Lohfink, "Die Erzählung vom Sündenfall," in *Das Siegeslied am Schilfmeer* (Frankfurt, 1965), 81–101.

Without this background of constant human failure, the New Testament message of salvation would fall on deaf ears. God's greatness consists in this, that he has loved mankind despite mankind's neglect, and has given up his only son (cf. Jn 3:16). Even after the coming of Christ, mankind's disposition did not change; as regards man, there is no pure and good world, no paradisiac "innocence," and all the talk about "unspoiled nature" is prone to lead us into a dangerous naturalism and amoralism. The fascinating achievements of the natural sciences in opening and developing the natural potential of the material world must not blind us to the fact that the moral dangers in the realm of human nature and personality are still with us. As a corrective to any optimistic theology of creation, such as would suit the modern temper, the theology of the Bible serves to recall the still unconquered distress of creation, and man's affinity to evil. All this has to be said before we may turn to that other vista, the view the Bible takes of the world as God's creation, the object of his kindness and love, his concern for salvation, and his will for the consummation.

THE GOD-CREATED WORLD CALLED TO THE NEW CREATION

That God created the world is an incontestable tenet of faith, adopted from Judaism, which is implied throughout the New Testament. Naturally enough, it is put into words only rarely. The clearest statement occurs in Paul's speech on the Areopagus: "The God who made the world and everything in it, being Lord of heaven and earth, does not live in shrines made by man" (Acts 17:24). God is frequently addressed as creator of the world in prayers and hymns, for example in the joint prayer of Acts 4:24: "Sovereign Lord who didst make the heaven and the earth and the sea and everything in them," and particularly in the hymn to the divine nature in Apocalypse 4:11: "Worthy art thou, our Lord and God, to receive glory and honor and power, for thou didst create all things, and by thy will they existed and were created." These words occur in the great vision of the throne, to which we shall come back. The fact of the creation is affirmed in the Christ hymns, thus in Colossians 1:15: "He is . . . the first-born of all creation; for in him all things were created, in heaven and on earth . . . all things were created through him and for him," or in John 1:3: "All things were made through him, and without him was not anything made that was made," or finally in Hebrews 1:2: "Through whom also he created the world." In the ancient formula in 1 Corinthians 8:6, both God and Christ are named: "For us there is one God, the Father, from whom are all things and for whom we exist, and one Lord, Jesus Christ, through whom are all things and through whom we exist." It is significant that the creation by God, the relation of the created world to God, and the course of the world in its dependence upon God (cf. also Rom 11:36) are all included in the praise; in this manner, all these matters sound not like a doctrinal assertion but like a consciously grasped truth. God is not a dead concept, but a living reality; we see him not as self-contained absolute Being but as an active power. God is in constant dynamic relation to the world.

Other passages mention only the "foundation of the world"[19] or "the beginning of creation" (Mk 10:6; 13:19; cf. Rom 1:20), in different contexts but always in a manner to echo God's superiority and majesty. Similarly with the expression "consummation of the world," which in Matthew alone occurs five times; it points not only to the end of the world, but also and even more emphatically to God's action in the world, or the new creation of the world.[20] The Bible never thinks of the world as self-sufficient and detached from God; the world

---

[19] Mt 25:34; Lk 11:50; Jn 17:24; Eph 1:4; Heb 4:3; 9:26; 1 Peter 1:20; Ap 13:8; 17:8.

[20] The idea of the eschatological new creation, which Matthew in the passage referred to renders with the Hellenistic παλιγγενεσία has been expressed as early as Is 65:17 and 66:22. It lives on among the Jews; cf. E. Sjöberg, "Wiedergeburt und Neuschöpfung im palästinischen Judentum," *Studia Theologica* 4 (1950), 44–85; the same, "Neuschöpfung in den Toten-Meer-Rollen," *ibid.*, 9 (1955), 131–136; G. Schneider, "Die Idee der Neuschöpfung beim Apostel Paulus und ihr religionsgeschichtlicher Hintergrund," *Trierer Theologische Zeitschrift* 69 (1959), 257–270, and *Neuschöpfung oder Wiederkehr?* (Düsseldorf, 1961); H.-W. Kuhn, *loc. cit.*, note 10, 75–78.

always remains in God's hands, under his design and action, even when it appears to have turned totally away from God. God, in the liturgical-poetic language of the Apocalypse, is "the Alpha and the Omega" (1:8), "the beginning and the end" (21:6). "Nature" and "history" cannot be separated; God, the power that sustains all things, is as active in the realm of physics and biology as in human history which, too, is moved by man's decisions yet never falls outside the will of God. There is thus no separation of "profane history" and "history of salvation," because God realizes and advances his thoughts in the history which outwardly seems made by man. God allows nature its laws, and man his free will, and still achieves his divine goals. Accordingly, it is entirely possible to study the world in terms of its immanent mechanism and its external history, and in this sense to practice human science; God is active in the depth of the forces of nature, and hidden in the decisions of men. It is possible to speak of an autonomy of the earthly-worldly realms, and of man's autonomy in his actions, and yet we cannot deny God's autonomy. God is and works in all things in such a way that they are sustained by him and tend toward him. Only when we have understood this fact can we hope to see fully the Biblical affirmation of the world (that is, of all created things) and of the world's history. Belief in God as the biblical revelation conceives him is the ultimate reason why the Bible can never reject the created world.

212

This fundamental view of the world, which stems from faith in God the creator and Lord of the world, is not put in question by that pessimistic concept of the "world" which we considered in the first section. That is a narrower concept, which is rooted in the historical situation of the time and, above all, is morally determined. We find it confirmed in the language of the New Testament; for while the same expression *kosmos* is at times used also for the world as creation,[21] most of the passages concerning the "theology of creation" employ a different phrase: either the Old Testament expression of "heaven and earth,"[22] or else the universalistic "all things." We must give special attention to these (τὰ) πάντα statements, for they have far-reaching theological significance.

When we read of "all things" which God had made or which were made through Christ, and again of "all things" in which God is at work and over which Christ rules in order to return them to God, we are dealing with two different situations that yet ultimately belong together to constitute a unified picture of God's relation to the world. There is good reason for the gospel of John to stress in the prologue (1:3) that "all things were made through him, and without him was not any-

---

[21] Cf. the expression "the foundation of the world" (see note 19, above); also Jn 1:10; 17:5; Acts 17:24; Rom 1:20.

[22] Acts 4:24; 14:15; 17:24; Ap 10:6; 14:7; cf. Col 1:16; Ap 5:13; further the statements about heaven and earth passing away, Mt 5:18, 24:35, and elsewhere.

thing made that was made"; and the same holds for the hymn to Christ in the Letters to the Colossians (1:16): "For in him all things were created, in heaven and on earth, visible and invisible, whether thrones or dominions or principalities or authorities—all things were created through him and for him." John's prologue probably,[23] and the Letter to the Colossians certainly,[24] is an expression of Christian resistance to false gnostic doctrines which pretended to keep certain areas of creation outside of Christ's universal creative jurisdiction. There is no such thing as a lower, evil material world created, as Marcion and other gnostics taught, by a demiurge, a lesser power than God, an evil principle; there is no such thing as demon powers ruling the visible world in independence of God's and Christ's sovereignty. All things are from the beginning under God's power, who has created the whole world (in Christ) and remains its Lord.

[23] Cf. R. Schnackenburg, *Das Johannesevangelium* I (Freiburg, 1965), 215.

[24] Underlying the Letter to the Colossians there is clearly a Jewish-gnostic false doctrine, in which the "world elements," probably angelic powers ruling the world (star spirits?) are venerated and overestimated; cf. G. Bornkamm, "Die Häresie des Kolosserbriefes," in *Theologische Literaturzeitung* 73 (1948), 11–20; H. J. Gabathuler, *Jesus Christus, Haupt der Kirche—Haupt der Welt* (Zurich-Stuttgart, 1965), especially 142 f., 146 ff.; see also the Commentaries.

This universal lordship of God expresses itself also in history: history takes its course in accordance with God's wondrous designs and hidden counsels for our salvations. Romans 11:33–36 makes the matter especially clear. After a section in which Paul traces the hidden ways of God's salvation which are hard to comprehend even for a faithful Christian, the Apostle bursts out in a passionate hymn in God's praise: "O the depths of the riches and wisdom and knowledge of God!" He chooses words from the Old Testament to tell how unsearchable are God's counsels, how inscrutable his ways, and then concludes with the doxology: "For from him and through him and to him are all things. To him be glory for ever. Amen." This expression "all things"—*ta panta* in Greek, with the article!—does not mean simply the universe, creation as such, but in this context means primarily God's workings in history which, by his hidden guidance, becomes the history of salvation. But the world as creation is also implied, as the words "from him" show; God is the principle, the ever active force, and the goal of creation and of history; and creation and history are here one. As W. Thüsing[25] has expressed it: "Paul does not conceive of creation in the sense that a static universe is brought into existence, but as an event, dynamic through and through, which has been creatively called to life and set in motion with things, beings, and people." And the words "through him"

[25] *Per Christum in Deum* (Münster, 1965), 228.

mean that "all things," that is, all "judgments" and "ways," do not only grow out of God's design and will but are also in every case effected by God.[26]

Thus the creation and the order of redemption are grasped in a single vision and fused into one at their goal ("to him"). There is no doubt that in the New Testament the soteriological aspect predominates. The writings in which the statements about "all things" are most frequent—the Letters to the Colossians and to the Ephesians—are concerned with the eschatological redemption of mankind and the return of all things to God's perfect dominion, the gathering home into his order.[27] That redemption and return is effected through and in Christ who was to reconcile "all things" to God, "whether on earth or in heaven" (Col 1:20), and in whom God wanted to unite "all things," "things in heaven and things on earth" (Eph 1:10). The most immediate sphere in which Christ exercises his divine rule is the Church, his body, "the fulness of him who fills all in all" (Eph 1:23). The Church is also the organ which God reaches out to all the realms of the created, historically evolved universe that is ruled by creaturely forces, to consummate his power and

[26] *Ibid.*, 229.

[27] Cf. O. Perels, "Kirche und Welt nach dem Epheser- und Kolosserbrief," *Theologische Literaturzeitung* 76 (1959), 393–400; F. Mussner, *Christus, das Alle und die Kirche* (Trier, 1955); H. Schlier, *Der Brief an die Epheser* (Düsseldorf, 1957), 64 f., 206 f.; B. Reiche, in *ThWNT* V (1954), 892 f.

truly fulfill all things (cf. Eph 3:9).[28] This movement which redeems and perfects the world has
been set in motion only through Christ and his act
of reconciliation, and is effective only since his
resurrection. He, the "first-born from the dead," is
the beginning, the principle and the head of mankind and world redeemed, "that in everything he
might be pre-eminent" (Col 1:18). God has "made
him the head over all things for the Church" (Eph
1:22). This means that he has been appointed and
made the head of "all things" (cf. vv. 20–22), yet
in such a manner that he has first of all been given
to the Church as its head (cf. Col 1:18; Eph 5:23),
and through the Church is to achieve more and
more his "headship" over all things (cf. Col 2:10,
19; Eph 4:15).[29] The texts cited, and the inten-

[28] Cf. J. Gewiess, "Die Begriffe πληροῦν und πλήρωμα
im Kolosser- und Epheserbrief," in *Vom Wort des
Lebens* (Munich, 1951), 128–141; H. Schlier, *loc.
cit.* 193 f.; G. Delling in *ThWNT* VI (1959), 290 f.

[29] The relation of Church and world under Christ's
rule is variously defined, depending on how the
κεφαλή statements are understood. According to the
song underlying Col 1:15–20, v. 18 ἡ κεφαλὴ τοῦ
σώματος seems to have referred originally to the
"world body" over which Christ is the "head"; but
Paul, by adding της ἐκκλησίας, referred the statement
to the Church. He does in any event see Church
and Universe as closely related. Cf. H. Schlier in
ThWNT III (1938), 679 ff.; V. Warnach, "Kirche
und Kosmos," in *Enkainia*, ed. H. Edmonds (Düsseldorf, 1956), 170–205; H. J. Gabathuler, *loc. cit.* (note
24, above), 150–181.

tional use of the expression "all things," show that the issue is always the whole created world, and it is no coincidence that these letters refer repeatedly in so many words to God and his creative act. The same God who has created all things also creates a new man and a new mankind (cf. Eph 2:15), and leads all things, beginning with the new man, to a new and perfect order. The same Christ through and for whom all things were created (Col 1:16), who is before all things and in whom all things hold together (Col 1:17), is also the beginning and the head of the renewed mankind and all things that have come home to God. Here creation is indirectly reconfirmed in its divine origin and divinely ordained order; the redemptive event in Christ does not rob it of that character, does not alienate it from it: that event leads creation back to its original form, and forward to its full formation.

In principle, these thoughts are contained already in an earlier letter of Paul, the First Letter to the Corinthians, in the passage in which Paul, speaking of the resurrection, offers an encompassing survey of the divine plan (15:24–28). Here, too, the references to "all things" predominate. God will put all his enemies under Christ's feet, the last enemy to be destroyed being death which is completely annihilated by the resurrection. And when God has subjected "all things" to Christ, then the Son himself will also be subjected to him who put all things under him, so that God "may be everything to every one" (v. 28). Whether

we understand this fulsome expression more as
a formula, or concretely in the sense that God
achieves complete dominion of all redeemed, created beings and in all cosmic spheres, W. Thüsing
has put the meaning very well: "God reigns first
from within his children who have opened themselves to him, and beyond them in the entire
κτίσις, which is drawn into the freedom of God's
children and which in this freedom of divine glory
also opens to God's royal power."[30]

The same fusion of the world of creatures, history, mankind, and the universe, the same focus
upon the goal of all that happens in the world, can
be observed again in a New Testament book that
has little relation to Paul's writings: the Revelation of John. In a prophetic spirit and apocalyptic
guise, the book offers consolation to hard-pressed
Christian communities by guiding them toward
the end of time, the goal of the history of salvation,
the perfection of all things. After the dramatic
description of the events surrounding the end of
the world, after Christ's eschatological victory over
the enemies of God, after the resurrection and
judgment (19:11–20:15), Chapter 21 turns to the
new creation and the perfection of God's kingdom.
"Then I saw heaven and a new earth; for the first
heaven and the first earth had passed away, and
the sea was no more. . . . And he who sat upon
the throne said, 'Behold, I make all things new'"
(21:1, 5). But even before the final drama runs its

---

[30] *loc. cit.*, 249 f.

course, the prophet has a vision of God's throne in heaven and experiences the meaning of all that happens in its heavenly reality (Chapter 4). This mighty vision of the throne, with its symbolic figures and meaningful songs in praise of God, creator and universal king, is particularly revelatory of the world view with which our inquiry is concerned. If it is correct that the four living creatures and the twenty-four elders personify the chorus of the Fathers, representatives of the community,[31] it means that the universe and all mankind, nature and history, are present and gathered at God's throne, in that union and unity which exists for God. They unite in praise of the creator of the world and Lord of history, because God is about to consummate his work. The living creatures sing the song of the seraphim as they do in the vision of the prophet Isaiah, praising God's glory that is filling the whole earth (Is 6:3), but with the significant variation: "Holy, holy, holy is the Lord God Almighty, who was and is and is to come" (Ap 4:8). And the chorus of the twenty-four elders praises God, who is to receive honor and power, as him who did create all things, and by whose will all things existed (Ap 4:11). The created world takes part in mankind's history which God is now leading toward its goal, and mankind recalls that it received everything from God the

---

[31] This view is developed further in my essay "Die Kirche in der Welt," *BZ* 11 (1967), 1–21, especially 14–21.

creator who is now bringing history to ultimate salvation. The movement from the creation to redemption to perfection is here completed, and all darkness and confusion dissolves in the light of the divine plan. The end, which is not destruction but a new creation, the consummation, reveals the hidden meaning of the world and the direction of history. This is how the believer sees the world—and only the believer can so see it: and a more optimistic world view cannot be imagined. We have thus arrived at an understanding of the world that looks like the very opposite of that idea of a dangerous and "evil" world of which we spoke.

THE TENSION IN THE CHRISTIAN'S RELATION TO THE WORLD

This tension that the two series of Bible statements will produce in the reader—shall we try to dissolve it by conceptual distinctions, by a clarification of the differentiated world view of the New Testament? It may be desirable, and to a degree possible, to do so. We have seen that the concept "this world" or "this eon" belongs to a certain tradition, and must be understood in a more limited sense. But in the New Testament itself no clear distinctions are made; its language shifts from "world" in the sense of creation, the universe, the arena of man's life, to "world" as an historically evolved formation, indeed a spiritual entity, a moral sphere that concerns man in his endeavor; and there are no ways to make clean distinctions in the Bible among these divers world views. All these things concern and indeed challenge every man—even the Christian—in his existence and his view of himself. Thus it will be advisable to note and remember all the various faces of "world" which the New Testament shows us. But that means that the Christian will never be relieved of tension and unrest in his experience of "world," that his encounters with the "world" may be both positive and negative.

The Christian world view has not changed much throughout its history. Earlier ages tended to emphasize more the Christian distance from the world; they were conscious of the dangers with which the world and its influences threaten man's salvation, in harmony with that foreground view of "world" which we encounter in many New Testament passages. The present age inclines more toward an open attitude to the world, in keeping with the modern mood of life and its urge to make the world wholly subservient; Christian theology can in this context point to God's command to man that he be creative, and to the incarnation of the Son of God which implies a divine confirmation and approval of the world of man. After centuries of a negative attitude toward the world in the name of the Christian faith and Christian striving for salvation, this new orientation is no doubt justified and desirable; but the divergent statements in the Bible do not thereby lose their justice and importance; indeed, they acquire greater significance in a time that practices a veritable worship of the "world." In his surrender to his work and the enjoyment of life, man forgets the humane and moral values he must realize to achieve happiness. With this in mind, we shall now look briefly at a few New Testament texts which can easily be misunderstood but which, seen in the proper perspective, carry a valid message for the Christian of today.

1 Corinthians 2:29-31 is a much discussed and variously interpreted passage: "I mean, brethren, the appointed time has grown very short; from now on, let those who have wives live as though they had none, and those who mourn as though they were not mourning, and those who rejoice as though they were not rejoicing, and those who buy as though they had no goods, and those who deal with the world as though they had no dealings with it. For the form of this world is passing away."[32] These remarks have been connected with Stoic thought, and it has been held that Paul was teaching a form of inner imperturbability (*ataraxia*), a disinterest in the things of the world, a cool reserve, an attitude as-if. Now it is certain that Paul desires a distance to the world; but to understand this desire rightly we must inquire into Paul's motives. Does he mean that the things of this world are worthless (gnostic deprecation) or that they are unimportant to man (stoic atti-

---

[32] On this passage see esp. W. Schrage, *loc. cit.*, note 1; G. Hierzenberger, Weltbewertung bei Paulus nach 1 Cor 7:29–31 (Düsseldorf, 1967).

tude)? In this context we must note that he writes under a specific eschatological aspect: the time has grown short, distress is impending (v. 26),[33] the form of this world is passing away—and the underlying image is that of an actor passing from the stage. Although Paul, moved by his immediate expectation of the parousia, may have a foreshortened and thus sharpened perspective, it is still valid in principle: this world does not endure —it approaches its end ineluctably though there may still be centuries to come; it is "perishable." Rightly understood, the word has a profound meaning; we cannot hold on to the things of the world, and it is foolish to cling to them as though they were of imperishable value. They are not by this attitude rendered completely worthless—on the contrary, they are now seen in their original created goodness, but are judged by their contingency and limitations. In the passage cited, Paul acknowledges that marriage is permitted and is good, he even defends it against a rigorism which would forbid marital relations (7:1 ff.). He is entirely serious in saying that we should buy and

[33] The expression ἐνεδτωσα ἀνάγκη can thus mean either an impending or a present distress. In terms of lexicon meaning, either is possible; cf. W. Bauer, *Griechisch-Deutsches Wörterbuch zu den Schriften den NT* (Berlin, 1958), 528. Bauer opts for the first meaning, but the overwhelming number of the occurrences in the New Testament argues rather for the second. The eschatological urgency is present in either case.

use the things of the world; but with his sharpened vision he sees that we cannot keep what we have bought, and cannot use up what we use. Accordingly, the expressions "mourn as though they were not mourning" and "rejoice as though they were not rejoicing" do not mean a rejection of human feelings and passions, do not mean that he is advocating a stoic apathy, but only this reservation that the sorrow and joy of this world pass away. The advice to the unmarried not to marry stands side by side with the advice to the married not to leave their spouses (v. 27); but even this is only advice, because Paul believes the *parousia* to be imminent; those who do not take the advice commit no sin (v. 28). The warning, therefore, to those who have wives, that they should act as though they had no wives cannot mean they should terminate their marriages; it can mean only that they should remain conscious that marriage is temporary. The entire warning has the character of an "eschatological reservation." As W. Schrage writes: "The ὡς μή does not mean that the Christian is not to commit himself and pursue his dealings with the world coolly, from a distance, and half-heartedly."[34] Paul only wishes to warn against the illusion that man could hold on to the things and joys of this world. Man does not have the final say in this world—God can take everything from him, because God decides the end of our bodily existence and the end of this world.

[34] W. Schrage, *loc. cit.*, 149.

The same theme, though in a different context and formulation, echoes in 1 John 2:17. The author here warns against love of the "world," which represents "the lust of the flesh and the lust of the eyes and the pride of life" (v. 15 f.). This moral caution might becloud the fact that the things of the earth are true goods, that man's instincts are God-given forces for good; but the evaluation of the world as perishable, preliminary, and penultimate remains: "The world passes away, and the lust of it; but he who does the will of God abides forever."

We finally recall those passages in which the Christians are called "exiles," "aliens," and "strangers" on earth.[35] They give an impression of unworldliness, and may often have been so interpreted. But happy pilgrimage in a world which is not our final abode, and which often depresses us, may also be a good image, and need not hamper us in our earthly tasks. According to 1 Peter 2:11 f., we "aliens and exiles" are not only to abstain from "the passions of the flesh" but are also to "maintain good conduct among the Gentiles." The prospect of the promises before us (cf. Heb 11:13) must not alienate us from this world, but is to give us the strength and courage with which to master our earthly tasks. There is much in the mood and

---

[35] 1 Peter 1:17; 2:11; Heb 11:13; the imagery of 2 Cor 5:6–8 is related. On the idea, cf. G. Stählin in *ThWNT* V (1954), 28–31; K. L. and M. A. Schmidt, *ibid.*, 850 f.

attitude of early Christianity that must assuredly be ascribed to the then prevailing mood of life; and we must remind ourselves of the oppressed situation of the communities, the reduced social position of the Christians, and the threat of persecution and disaster. But after discounting all time-conditioned aspects, and listening only to the way in which the faithful judged the world, and to the motives for Christian conduct in the world, we shall still hear ideas that retain their validity for our age as well.

In his relation to the world, the Christian remains in a constant tension. He stands midway between possession and the loss of this world's goods, between service to this world and distance to it, between enjoyment and renunciation. In his existence, bound as it is to the existing world and threatened by death and annihilation, there never exists a stable order in his relation to the world— only a day-to-day renewed decision, a dynamic stance. The Christian's relation to the world is dialectical: being God's good creation, it attracts him and appeals to him; but being a historical world that must ultimately perish, it offers him no lasting home (cf. Heb 13:14), no ultimate fulfillment of his life (cf. 2 Cor 4:18; 5:6). The Christian can and must perform his earthly vocation in the world, and that includes marriage, family, and society; but he can and must also fulfill his vocation as a Christian whose ultimate goal is God. Thus he is the citizen of two worlds—not in a state of divided consciousness but in a state of living and dynamic tension, always asked that he does not forget the one for the other. He will avoid flight from the world as much as obsession with the world; his fundamental attitude will always be Christian freedom: "All things are yours, and you are Christ's, and Christ is God's" (1 Cor 3:22 f.).

Index

A

Abraham, 72, 87, 163
Acts of the Apostles, on conversion, 50
Adam and Eve, 11
Apocalypse, 66, 212
  sermon on repentance, 65
Areopagus (*see* Saint Paul)
Atheism, 92
  problem of, 93n
Augustine, Saint, 24, 153

B

Baptism, 14–15, 52, 202
  of repentance, 41–42
Beatitudes, 143–144
Benedict, Saint, monastic family, 188
Bible,
  concept of perfection, 159–161
  faith, 71
  fundamental belief, 23
  historical setting of man, 16–19
  integral view of man, 7, 10
  man's future, 18
  meaning and direction for man, 3
  natural community of man, 12

salvation or perdition, 27
  on truth of God's revelation, 70
  view of the "world," 211–212
Book of the Dead of the Mandaeans, 204
  and demonic world, 206
Bourgeois morality, 128
Bultmann, Rudolf, *Jesus and the Word*, 135

C

Christ,
  antitype of first Adam, 15
  bearer of God's salvation, 148
  call for conversion, 44–45
  concept of faith, 80
  conquest of Jewish dualism, 203
  and discipleship, 99–101
  on growth of faith, 83–84
  "light of the world," 115–116, 125
  meaning of "imitation" of, 102–114
  salvation, 57–58
  Second Adam, 121
Christology,
  concentration, 58
  confession of faith, 82

Index

Church, exerciser of Divine Rule, 216
Conversion, 47–49, 54–66
  answer to Jesus' message, 36
  defined, 46
  and faith, 56–60
  fundamental summons to man, 34
  gift of God, 55
  Jewish guilt, 52–53
  moral, 50
  necessity for salvation, 43
  religious, 51
  total transformation of man, 34

D

Dialectic, relation of Christian to world, 227
Diaspora, 92
Discipleship, 99–100
  according to Saint John, 115–116, 118
Divorce, 174–175
Dualism, 29
  New Testament writings, 193–194
  in pagan-Hellenistic world, 203–204
  primacy of spirit, 6
Dupont, J., 168

E

Early Church, on Jesus' eschatological appeal, 20–21
Eichrodt, W., 26
Equality, core of Christ's message, 13
Eschatology (*also* eschatological, eschatologicalism), 172, 201

Christian perfection, 173–175
God's . . . judgment, 63–64
New Testament ethics, 147
thesis of, 146
virtues, 66
Evangelic Counsels, God's call to individual, 186–189
Evil, basic to man's history, 208

F

Faith,
  biblical, 71–72
  concept of, 80
  content, 68
  and testimony, 81–82
  testing of, 86–88
Fall of Man, starting point in history, 18
Freedom, 23
  Christian, 228
  in God, 2

G

Gentiles, 226
  and conversion, 53–54, 155
Gnostic (*also* gnosticism), 29, 204–205
  Saint John's Prologue, 214
  symbolic equations of, 206
Grace, 49
  faith as gift of, 90

H

Hermetic, writings on gnosticism, 206–207
Herkenrath, J., 182
"Historicity" of man, 2n
Holy Spirit, 54–55, 59, 97–98, 157

I

Imitation of Christ,
"being in Christ," 122–124
hope of eternal life, 126–127
part of one's vocation, 124
through faith, 125–126
true meaning, 108
"Ingathering movement," 103–104
"Interim State," of body and soul, 8
Isaiah, 141, 220
as "prophet of faith," 76–77

J

John the Baptist, Saint, 33–34, 37
necessity for conversion, 38
salvation through faith, 57–58
spokesman for New Testament, 40
John the Evangelist, Saint, 64–65, 226
on discipleship, 115–116, 118
faith of Martha, 80–81
growth and life of faith, 87–88
Prologue, 213–214
salvation, 21–22
summary on faith, 98
unbelief in Jesus, 96–97
Jonah, 43
Judgment,
defined, 8
final, 38

K

Klausner, J., 131–132

L

Lamb on Mount Zion, idea of fellowship, 119–120
Last Supper, 155, 188

M

Man,
distinction of soul and body, 9
freedom and perfection of, 23
God-given existence, 5
as "historical" being, 17
image of God, 6, 10, 14
perfection of, 11
two views of happiness, 23–24
Manicheism, 205
Marcion (the gnostic), 214
Mary (Virgin Mother), her faith, 74
Messiah, 38
Judaism and Christianity contrast, 203
judgment, 40
in Matthew, 39
Metanoia (change of mind), and penance, 35
Saint Paul's statement, 55
Mount Sinai, theophany on, 74

N

"New Man" (*see* Saint Paul)
New Testament,
dualistic thought, 193–194
ethics, 147
and faith, 77–83
insights on imitation of Christ, 122–127
pessimistic concept of world, 190–191

problems of faith, 91–92
for today's Christians, 223–228
"world view" of man, 192

O

Old Covenant, and books of revelation, 208
Old Testament,
concept of perfection, 162–167
examples of faith, 84–85
and faith, 72–77
Original Sin, effects, 17–18

P

Parousia, 21, 62, 94, 224–225
Paul, Saint, 21, 51, 56
concept of followership, 120–122
concept of Two Eons, 199–200
divine plan, 218
faith of Abraham, 89
imitation of Christ, 122–124
Metanoia, 55
"new man," 15, 218
salvation through faith, 72–73
sermon on Areopagus, 53, 210
social bond of Man, 13–14
Stoic thought clarified, 223–225
summary of faith, 98
Penance, 34
in Old and New Testaments, 36
Perfection, Christian (*also* perfection),
biblical concept, 159–161

essence of, 159
gift of God, 176–177
and *Imitation of Jesus,* 184–186
in Matthew's Gospel, 169–172
poverty, chastity and obedience, 187–188
reflecting salvific reality, 173
Peter, Saint,
Imitatio Christi, 117
in Pentecostal sermon, 52
on repentance, 51, 53
Pharisees, 37, 48, 95, 178, 197
and Publican, 44–45
Plöger, O.,
on apocalyptic world view, 196
Poverty, chastity and obedience, in light of evangelic counsels, 187–188
Prayer of Petition, 177

Q

Qumran, 100
future salvation, 201
on perfection, 164–165, 167

R

Rabbinism, 198
Radical Pacificism, 138
Redemption, 55, 216
Resurrection, 9, 27, 29, 121
interim state, 8
Revelation, 19
and salvation, 69

S

Sadducees, 9, 29, 197
Salvation, 19, 22, 29, 69

belief in bodily resurrection, 205
and conversion, 37, 43, 47
definitive, 142
through faith, 57
in the New Testament, 150–151
Sermon on the Mount, 143, 146
Schmid, J., 183
Schoeps, H. J., Sermon on the Mount, 132–133
"School of Disciples," 104
Schrage, W., 225
Schweizer, E., 118
Scriptures, as historical statement of faith, 69
Sermon on the Mount,
Apostalic Fathers, 137–138
applied by evangelists, 150–152
Christian perfection, 173–174
full salvation, 143
fundamental demands, 153
Jesus' moral teachings, 154–157
Jesus' radicalism, 139
language of, 149–150
liberal interpretation, 134
manifesto to all men, 148
modern existential theology, 136
in Saint Matthew, 169–171
Sex, Jesus' attitude, 156

Sheol, (realm of the dead), 27–28

T

Theology, moral, and state of perfection, 158
of creation, 213
Thomas à Kempis, 101
Thüsing, W., 219,
on Saint Paul and Creation, 215–216
Tolstoi, Count Leo, 138
Torah,
righteousness and perfection, 163–164
on Sermon on the Mount, 131
Two Eons, Doctrine of, 198–199
as expressed by Christians, 200–201

W

Windisch, H., *The Meaning of the Sermon on the Mount,* 133–134

Y

Yahweh, 37, 75
creation, 4
idea of "soul," 16
Yahvistic view of history, 207

Z

Zaccheaeus, 43